Christmas, 1993

For Effie —
    May you always cherish the memories
of your "Journey of Faith" with our dear
Blessed Mother.

                        Love,
                        Ann

The Triumph
OF THE
Immaculate Heart

UT Adveniat Regnum Christi
Adveniat Regnum Mariae

St. Louis Grigon de Montfort

The Triumph
OF THE
Immaculate Heart

*"In the end
my Immaculate Heart will triumph.
Russia will be converted
and a period of peace will be
given to the world"*

The Blessed Virgin Mary at Fatima
October 13, 1917

JANICE T. CONNELL

With an introduction by Father Rene Laurentin
Photography by Larry Galloway ©

Our Lady Queen of The Cosmos, Saint Sulpice Church, Paris

The Triumph of The Immaculate Heart
© 1993 by Janice T. Connell. All Rights Reserves.

Library of Congress Catalog Card No. 93-84748

Illustration and Design: *Janet Schaefer*
Printing: *Day & Night Graphics, Carpinteria • CA*

Published by:
Queenship PUBLISHING COMPANY
P.O. Box 42028 • Santa Barbara, CA 93140-2028
Phone (800) 647-9882 FAX 805-569-3274

Printed in the United States of America

ISBN: 1-882972-11-2

O JESUS, KING OF ALL NATIONS, MAY YOUR REIGN BE RECOGNIZED ON EARTH

1990

CONSECRATION
AND
DEDICATION

*This book is consecrated
to the Immaculate Heart of Mary
in gratitude for the gift of the Incarnation.*

*My family and I dedicate this book to the
Lord Jesus Christ, King of all Nations
with great love.*

This Icon, of Christ The King, was transported to Russia as part of the Victorious Queen of The World Peace Pilgrimage of Thanksgiving in October 1992. It was placed in Red Square before the open Chapel where the Basilica of Our Lady of Kazan is being rebuilt. The original Basilica was destroyed in 1917 by the Soviets as a sign to the Russian people that God does not exist.

Chaplet of Unity in Honor of Jesus as True King of All Nations
*"To those special souls who honor Me in this devotion
I promise to grant My Kingly Blessings, My Mercy,
Pardon and Protection."*
(see page 78)

Pilgrim Statue of Our Lady of Fatima

Contents

ACKNOWLEDGEMENTS

The Most Holy Trinity ever present.

The Blessed Virgin Mary, and her Divine Son
for their guidance and assistance with St. Joseph, in these times.

Pope John Paul II for his faithfulness as he leads people toward the Triumph of the Immaculate Heart.

Father Rene Laurentin, great Twentieth Century theologian
who has heroically guarded the integrity of Marian dogma and tradition.

My family and especially William Troy Connell, my son, for his editorial skills which he graciously brought to this manuscript.

John A. Haffert for his leadership and dedication to Our Lady of Fatima,
and for his generosity in sharing his knowledge for the purposes of this book.

Dr. Rosalie Turton for her faith and steadfastness.

Larry Galloway whose photography brings the Peace Pilgrimage of Thanksgiving to Russia
to all those whose hearts are united with Our Lady of Fatima.

The Peace Pilgrims who helped me prepare this book, especially The Don Ralph Family.

The 940 Peace Pilgrims who made the Peace Pilgrimage on behalf of
all those on earth who sincerely desire peace.

All the children of Mary, Mother of God for whom this book is intended.

8

INTRODUCTION

When I addressed the Peace Pilgrims at Fatima as they were preparing for their flight to Russia to honor Our Lady as Victorious Queen, I told them this story of the miracle of the Icon of the Czarina of Russia.

On February 13, 1917, seven months before the Revolution of October, a farm women Eudoxie from Potchinok heard a mysterious voice and saw a beautiful icon in her sleep.

"In Kolomonskoe the red icon must be established."

She was afraid to go to her priest. Our Lady appeared to her, on February 26, making the same request.

The priest of Kolomonskoe (in the suburb of Moscow) had only a black icon and did not know the red one. He showed her the icons venerated by the church, but none of them resembled the one in the dream. He then had the basement searched where a large icon was found of the Queen of Heaven, draped in a cloth of purple, with a specter and globe, and the Child in her lap.

Eudoxie's visit to the church happened on the day of the abdication of the Czsar; March 2, 1917 shortly before his arrest on March 20, 1917. Fatima's first apparition occurred on the following May 13, 1917. Since that March, the icon of Our Lady, as the new Queen and Czarina of Russia had become itinerant, in churches and monasteries,

On August 22, 1990, the last communist Putsch of 1990 in Moscow was finished. This was the *Feast of The Queenship of Mary,* so the Russians now could believe that Our Lady would always be <u>their</u> Queen.

This century comes to an end, people all over the world are becoming aware of the universal Queenship of the Blessed Virgin Mary. Her apparitions have multiplied to all corners of the earth. I have investigated and written extensively about these apparitions.

The central theme of all these apparitions of our Lady is the Gospel message of Conversion. The mission of the Blessed Virgin is that of Mother to our world. The urgency of all contemporary

apparitions portends a serious historical turning point at the threshold of the Third Millennium. The Blessed Virgin's messages to visionaries is: "The world is in danger. Humanity is destroying itself by abandonment to sin. Love, pray, fast, and do penance."

The Victorious Queen Peace Pilgrimage is an opportunity for everyone to demonstrate love and self-sacrifice. It is mystically linked to the prophesies from the Blessed Mother at Fatima, Medjugorje and Grovecho. Our Lady said at Medjugorje, in the way of Fatima, "Russia is the people in which God will be most glorified." (October 1981). This Peace Pilgrimage chronicled herein is for all those who seek Peace.

I have been studying Marxism since 1939. I have been following religious events for the past 30 years with trips in more than 40 countries, including eastern block countries. With that knowledge, I believe that people all over the world who love, pray and sacrifice will help Our Lady to bring peace into the world. God needs human action to effect human salvation. The pilgrimage from Fatima to Russia actualizes the predictions of Fatima. It is a stage of goodwill on the Road of Peace, from darkness to light for everyone.

Professor René Laurentin Ph.D., S.T.D.

PARIS, FRANCE

10

The Eternal Mother of God

Photo by anonymous Pilgrim

Prologue

The Eternal Mother

Mary Mediatrix of all Grace

My role as Victorious Queen is an Incarnational Event.

Through the Eternal Father's will all creation is subject to my command.

His children of the earth belong to me in a relationship which is now being disclosed.

Through Jesus all things of the earth are subject to me for the use of my children's salvation.

Like God, I bow before my children's freedom.

The day will come when my children will understand that through Jesus I have all the goods of the earth to give them.

As the Mother of their Eternal Life I am juridical in the disposal of gifts to my children.

I am always present to all my children.

I never leave the presence of any of my children.

Every action of their life is committed in my presence and the presence of God.

Soon all God's children of the earth will become aware of that truth.

Pilgrimages free my children's souls from their attachments to the earth.

Wherever I am sent on apparition, there is immense grace for those who choose to participate.

I am always present in a special way for those who visit my dear Son Jesus in the Blessed Sacrament.

PART I

Vision

It shall come to pass in the last days, says God, that I will pour out a portion of my spirit upon all mankind: Your sons and daughters shall prophesy, your young men shall see visions, your old men shall dream dreams. Indeed, upon my servants and my handmaids I will pour out a portion of my spirit in those days, and they shall prophesy. And I will work wonders in the heavens above, and signs on the earth below: blood, fire, and a cloud of smoke. The sun shall be turned to darkness, and the moon to blood, before the coming of that great and glorious day of the Lord. Then shall everyone be saved who calls on the name of the Lord.

Acts 2: 17-21

The Holy Rosary

SEVEN GREAT BLESSINGS

In *the Secret of The Rosary* (p. 65), St. Louis De Montfort states:
"The Rosary recited with meditation on the mysteries brings about the following marvelous results:

It gradually gives us a perfect knowledge of Jesus Christ;
it purifies our souls, washing away sin;
it gives us victory over all enemies;
it makes it easy for us to practice virtue;
it sets us on fire with love of Our Blessed Lord;
it enriches us with graces and merits;
it supplies us with what is needed to pay all our debts to
God and to our fellow men, and finally, it obtains all kinds
of graces for us from Almighty God."

THE ROSARY AND CONVERSION

"If you say the Rosary faithfully until death, I do assure you that, in spite of the gravity of your sins 'you shall receive a never fading crown of glory.' Even if you are on the brink of damnation, even if you have one foot in hell, even if you have sold your soul to the devil as sorcerers do who practise black magic, and even if you are a heretic as obstinate as a devil, sooner or later you will be converted and will amend your life and save your soul, if - and mark well I say - if you say the Holy Rosary devoutly every day until death for the purpose of knowing the truth and obtaining contrition and pardon for your sins."

-St. Louis De Monfort
The Secret of the Rosary (p. 12)

14

CHAPTER I

Apparitions

Reign of Love

*Apparitions are more a function of
hope than faith.*

The Mother of God
Gamaeil art from the Basilica at Lourdes, France

Archbishop Dominic Tang S.J. spent 22 years in a Chinese Communist prison. His only weapon for survival was the rosary, which he prayed continuously. After his jailer confiscated his rosary he used his fingers to count the decades.

As the twentieth century draws to a close, Marian apparitions are occurring with a frequency and urgency heretofore unparalled in Christianity. From the jungles of Panama to the rural hills of Rowanda, Africa; from deep within China, South America and Canada and in Europe, Syria, Ukraine, Slavakia, Korea, the United States, Ireland, England, India, the Philippines, Vietnam and Australia, people claim to see the Blessed Virgin Mary, or hear her. Some even claim to see and hear the Lord Jesus Christ.

What is an apparition? St. Thomas Aquinas taught that apparitions are more a function of hope than faith. They involve prophesy and give a preview of what the future will be. 1 "If God... decides to send His Son, or Our Lady to repeat with signs of fire and light that which (mankind) has forgotten, to convert us, to involve us prophetically in the history of salvation, that is urgent news, marking a turning point for the world."2

People from all walks of life and many different faiths have responded to the proliferation of apparitions in this century by increasing their prayer life, by fasting several times a week on bread and water, by spiritual and corporal works of mercy and by almsgiving. In these times people all over the world are learning the immense power of the rosary.

The rosary is ... "A school of holiness for those who are willing to learn its lessons." 3

Pope Leo XIII in his encyclical on the rosary, LEATITAE SANCTAE, deplores three pernicious tendencies at work to bring society to a low ebb.

Distaste for a simple and laborious life. Abhorrence to suffering of any kind. Forgetfulness of a future life.

His remedy: "The rosary which consists in a fixed order of prayer combined with devout meditation on the life of Christ and the Blessed Mother."

Pilgrimages to holy sites, conferences, and special places of worship have become a preferred means of spiritual renewal as people travel to even such extraordinary shrines as Medjogorje in the heart of war ravaged Bosnia. The Basilica in Mexico City is another favorite for it houses the image of the Blessed Virgin Mary which was miraculously given to Juan Diego in the mid 16th century. Extensive scientific investigation has concluded that the image upon the Tilma is indeed not possibly of the earth. The Tilma of Juan Diego bears the only divine image of the Blessed Virgin Mary that is known in these times.

Pilgrims with the Pilgrim Icon of Our Lady of Guadalupe which they are escorting on its first journey to Red Square in Moscow. The Icon is also known as Our Lady of The Americas.

In Portugal the faith has always been strong. Mary, the Mother of God, appeared there in a small, remote village known as Fatima on 13 May 1917 to three young children.4 There were six more apparitions at Fatima. The faithful throughout the world eventually heard the frightening messages to the three children, Lucia, Francesco and Jacinta by the Blessed Virgin.

The predictions of Our Lady of

Fatima involved a second world war, if the world did not immediately return to prayer and penance. The Blessed Virgin said:

I am the Queen of the Holy Rosary. Ask my faithful children to return to the rosary at once. So many lives will be destroyed because people do not pray. They do no penance.

The Blessed Virgin showed the

children hell. She explained that many beloved children of God end up in hell because they have no one to pray and do penance for them. The Blessed Mother spoke about a reign of terror beginning in Russia and spreading to the whole world. This amazed those who heard the messages of the ignorant shepherd children of Fatima because Russia was too poor and primitive in those days to feed its own inhabitants let alone influence those beyond its borders. Who could foresee the savagery of the Soviet regime about which the Blessed Mother warned mankind? She explained that if people continued to refuse to live the Gospel, Russia, unjustly governed, would spread its terrors throughout the world.

But she also promised:

In the end my Immaculate Heart will triumph and an era of peace will be granted to the world.

During the last seventy-five years, millions of people of all races, and many beliefs have responded in various ways to the messages of the Mother of Jesus Christ, given to the world at Fatima, Portugal. At that time in Europe, the horrors and suffering caused by World War I were reality, for the war did not end until November, 1917. Not only was the Mother of Jesus Christ speaking at Fatima of yet

The great shrine of Our Lady of Fatima on the 75th anniversary of the final apparition, October 13, 1992 (note dove in flight)

another world war, but she also spoke there of the "annihilation of nations."

The Blessed Virgin showed visions of hell to the innocent little Portuguese shepherd children: 7 year old Jacinta, her 8 year old brother Francesco, and her 11 year old cousin Lucia. So shocking were the horrors of hell that Jacinta never recovered from the memory.

The Blessed Virgin reminded the children:
Many of God's children go to hell because there is no one to pray for them.

Jacinta suffered much and died within two years of the visions. When her body was exhumed recently in preparation for the seventy-fifth anniversary of the Fatima apparitions, it was found incorrupt.

Seventy-five years after the apparitions in Fatima, the world is a powder keg. Unemployment in England in 1993 broke through the three million barrier for only the second time this century. Prince Charles, heir to the throne of England, told his subjects of the need for a spiritual dimension in a technicological age.

Millions are dying in the 1990's in Somalia as U. S. Marines have been deployed to assist the starving with international food supplies and necessities. Amid the abundances of the earth, starvation is a sad fact for some. There is a brutal war in Bosnia. The City of Sarajevo (where World War I began) has been under siege and according to the news reports, people there froze and starved to death in the winter of 1993. Concentration camps, rape camps, and ethnic cleansings in the region are internationally reported. Does the world know? Does the world care? Some ask: Does God know? Does God care?

In Bosnia on June 24, 1981, on the feast of John the Baptist, the Blessed Virgin Mary is reported to have been sent by God to begin daily apparitions that continue to this day. Six young shepherd children in the village of Medjugorje quote the words of the Blessed Mother:

Hurry and be converted.

The urgency of the messages at Medjugorje is chilling. Allegedly, this daily visitation of the Blessed Virgin is her last apparition on earth for she tells the visionaries that after the ten secrets she has given are realized she will not need to come to earth again. The visionaries of Mejugorje quote the Blessed Mother:

Prayer and fasting will stop war.
It will change the natural law.

Who could foresee the devastating civil war in Bosnia in 1981? Our Lady calls herself the Queen of Peace at Medjugorje. Will people respond to her messages? Will the war in Bosnia spread to the whole world? Experts speak of the apparitions at Medjugorje as the Fatima Peace Place in Action.5

The Queen of Peace
is God's most loving gift to all His children.
She brings Eternal Life to all His lost children.
She is His most faithful, most trusted servant.
Her love for all His children is God's love.
God's will is that now
all people throughout His world
know the Plan He has
to restore His Kingdom on earth.
His most beloved creature,
Mary,
the Mother He has given to all His creatures
through His Son Jesus,
brings His Plan to our globe now.
She does only God's will.
Mary is virtue.
All God's children
are called to be like her.
All are called to accept the great Plan
she brings from God,
to restore His Kingdom on earth.

19

How are the apparitions at Fatima relevant today, especially in the light of Medjugorje?

A reasonable understanding of the significance of Fatima's messages to the world rests in the Old Testament prophecies that continuously call for people to amend their lives, to pray and do penance. The prophets of Fatima were the three children who faithfully reported the messages of the Mother of God to, for the most part, an unbelieving world. Some heeded the messages from heaven. Most did not and World War II came storming across the planet followed by a mad arms race which has left the earth toxic, and mankind bloated with theories and ideas that do not satisfy the deepest longings of the human heart.

John Haffert in his insightful book, *To Prevent This,* explains that the modern day mystic Martha Robin who lived 30 years solely on the Eucharist proclaimed:

"This atom bomb! When one thinks that small nations will also have it and only two fools will be needed to destroy everything."

Dr. J. Paul McNally worked on the first atom bomb. In his book *State of Emergency,* AMI Press, he advised that even two or three of the more

than 50,000 superbombs now ready for use could cause nuclear holocaust.[6]

History records the human tendency to follow a path of ever increasing destruction. The Gospel message is the antidote. Jesus teaches that the mercy of God is above all His works. Since humanity is a work of the Divine Mind, the Savior of mankind is God's Infinite Mercy. It is through prayer that mankind accesses the Divine. It is through fasting that humanity has the strength to live. Ivan Dragicevic of Medjugorje speaks often of the Blessed Mother's message to the world about prayer and fasting. According to Ivan the Blessed Mother said, "Prayer without fasting is like a one-legged warrior. He is easily defeated."[7]

In this century the children of God are hearing through Lucia, the sole living visionary of Fatima, some inside details concerning the relationship between Jesus and His Mother Mary, and the people of the earth.

Many have asked Lucia why the Lord required the consecration of Russia by the Pope in conjunction with all the Bishops of the world. Lucia responded that Our Lord insisted

upon it for this reason:

I want My entire Church to know that this favor (the conversion of Russia) was obtained through the Immaculate Heart of My Mother so that it may extend this devotion of the First Five Saturdays later on and put the devotion to her Immaculate Heart beside the devotion to My Sacred Heart.[8]

Many people, including some Bishops and priests, however, accept neither apparitions nor private revelation. The consecration requested by the Fatima apparitions therefore did not occur until after some startling coincidences occurred in the life of Pope John Paul II.

One day as he bent down to bless a small girl who held a photo of Our Lady of Fatima, he narrowly missed death as an assassin shot him. After surgery, and a painful recovery, the Holy Father journeyed to the great Shrine of Fatima where he consecrated Russia and, in fact, the entire world to the Immaculate Heart of Mary on March 25, 1984. The visionary Lucia, later said that the Lord had accepted the collegiality of all the Bishops who joined with the Holy Father in this consecration. It was only then that the Iron Curtain began

to crumble.

Seventy five years have passed since the fateful messages of Fatima. The planet earth bears the scars of the nuclear reign of terror while nuclear weapons are hidden in the bowels of the earth.

On December 8, 1987, the leaders of the bi-polar balance of terror were receiving messages allegedly from the Mother of Jesus Christ through another visionary from another rural farming village, Medjugorje in the then Republic of Yugoslavia. Marija Pavlovic, through the good offices of U.S. Ambassador Alfred Klingon, delivered messages to both President Gorbachev of the Union of Soviet Socialist Republics and to President Ronald Reagan of the United States. 9

Civil disorder, civil war, financial instability, scarcity and even starvation, as well as ethnic cleansing, concentration camps, and rape camps are some of the early fruits of the meltdown of the Iron Curtain. But churches, closed for almost half a century, are opened once again. Four generations of the Soviet population lived under a godless regime in which atheism was the state imposed behavior pattern rigidly enforced upon all. It was often sanctioned by torture, poverty and death. None of these methods extinguished the faith of the people.

With the collapse of the Iron Curtain the rigidity collapsed too. Also the government. Who knows how the former Soviet Empire will evolve?

21

Hiroshema six weeks after the bomb.
America's response to the Japanese sneak attack at Pearl Harbor, Hawaii, on 7 December 1941 at 7:10 AM.

ROSARY NOVENA
The Novena that never fails

This novena consists of reciting five decades of the Rosary each day for 27 days in petition; then immediately five decades each day for 27 days in thanksgiving, whether or not the request has been granted.

History and Promise: The novena originated when Fortuna Agrelli, a girl of Naples, had suffered intense pain for 13 months. On February 16, 1884, she and her relatives began a novena of Rosaries for her recovery. Sitting on a high throne with the Infant Jesus on her lap, the Blessed Mother appeared to Fortuna on March 3. She held a Rosary in her hand and was accompanied by St. Dominic and St. Catherine of Sienna.

   Fortuna petitioned Our Lady, "Queen of the Holy Rosary, be gracious to me, restore me to health..." The Blessed Virgin replied, "... You have invoked me by various titles and have always obtained favors from me. Now, since you have called me by the title so pleasing to me, 'Queen of the Holy Rosary,' I can no longer refuse the favors that you petition; for this name is most precious and dear to me. Make three novenas, and you will obtain all."

   After Fortuna was cured, Our Lady appeared again. This time she said, "Whosoever desires to obtain favors from me should make three novenas of the prayers of the Rosary in petition and three novenas in thanksgiving."

   The miracle is said to have made a very deep impression on Pope Leo XIII, who urged all Christians to love the Rosary and say fervently.

Nihil Obstat: Rev. Terry Tekippe
Censor Librorum
Imprimatur: Most Rev. Francis B. Schulte
Archbishop of New Orleans
December 29, 1989

22

CHAPTER II

Victorious Queen

of The World

St. Catherine Laboure prayed for much of her life that Our Lady would be hailed as Queen of the World. She prophesied: "It will be a time of joy, triumph and prosperity. She will be carried like a banner and make a tour of the world."[1]

The Pilgrim Statue of Our Lady of Fatima is transported in procession by the faithful in Paris, France.

940 pilgrims gather in front of the Basilica at Lourdes, France. (See Galloways' panoramic joining of two plates to include all the pilgrims.)

Pilgrims from around the world assembled in Paris seventy five years after the first apparition of the Blessed Virgin Mary at Fatima to begin a pilgrimage to Moscow that St. Maximillan Kolbe spoke of in 1917. Many people of all faiths, or of no particular faith, hope that pilgrimage marks the beginning of the Triumph promised by the Blessed Virgin

Mary at Fatima when she said: "In the *"In the end my Immaculate Heart will triumph, Russia will be converted, and an era of peace will be given to the world."*

The 940 pilgrims on the Peace Flight all felt a deep call to be part of the historic journey. The suffering each endured is known to them and God alone. All was offered as an act of reparation to the Immaculate Heart of Mary for the conversion of the world. There was a broken hip in Paris. Another pilgrim had double pneumonia. Eddy Waldbilling and his brother Fritz shared a room. Eddy woke up with chest pains in Russia. His brother Fritz describes what happened:

"Suddenly Eddy turned and looked intently into the corner of the room. I looked to see what had drawn his attention and I saw two hands like a beam of light reach down to Eddy and the same light seemed to go from Eddy's hands reaching up and out of his body. And in that moment he was gone!" 2 He had died.

Two 747 plane loads of prayer warriors made the commitment to escort the Pilgrim Statue of Our Lady of Fatima, the Jesus King of All Nations Icon and the Tilma replica Icon of Our Lady of Guadalupe to Russia. The Peace Pilgrimage included holy sites in France, Portugal, Czechoslovakia, Poland, and finally to Red Square in Moscow. Here in front

One of the two transports chartered for the Peace Pilgrimage of Thanksgiving to Russia.

of armed militia at the site of Lenin's tomb, a small statue of Our Lady was symbolically crowned Victorious Queen of Heaven and Earth and particularly Queen of Russia. The date was October 18, 1992. Bishop Paolo Hnilica, titular Bishop of Russia was present. It was midnight. The rain was torrential as the pilgrims, in soaking blue jackets, escorted the small statue of Our Lady into Red Square. They recited the rosary in front of Lenin's tomb. As the rosary was concluded a crown was placed upon the statue of Our Lady. Suddenly the rain

Pilgrims endure hardship with great joy. They know the value of penance.

The Pilgrim Statue if Our Lady of Fatima en route to Red Square in Moscow, October 18, 1992. The Peace Pilgrims converged on Red Square. The rain was heavy at the changing of the guard in front of Lenin's tomb where the crowning of the Pilgrim Statue occurred. The rain immediately stopped above the statue. It rained every where else. The faithful are joyful in Russia. They have been liberated from militant atheism by prayer. (Photo by annonimous pilgrim.)

that it will be saved only through the Immaculate Heart of His Mother for Jesus entrusted peace to her. 3

From approximately 250 AD to 1100 AD, Church Fathers of the East and West vied with each other in extolling the merits and dignity of the Blessed Mother, calling her: "more pure than the angels, the all-holy Blessed Virgin, by nature more beautiful, more graceful and more holy than the Cherubim and Seraphim themselves and the whole host of angels." Their love for the Blessed Mother was manifested in deeds as well: "Churches were dedicated to the Immaculate Virgin and masses were celebrated for the glory of God in honor of the Virgin." 4

stopped. There was an astonished silence for each knew that the rain also suddenly stopped 75 years earlier when the Blessed Virgin appeared in her final apparition at Fatima. The people in the crowd began looking around. Was the Blessed Virgin there at Red Square? Some say they saw her there. All said they knew she was present.

Bishop Hnilica cried out to the exuberant pilgrims, "The Triumph of the Immaculate Heart has begun." It was then that the Russian onlookers began to embrace the pilgrims. Surely the Mother of all people was smiling. The pilgrims came to Russia with six tons of Rosaries, Bibles, holy cards, and religious books. Five Bishops, twenty three priests, self-proclaimed visionaries, men and women of different faiths and levels of beliefs formed the coterie of pilgrims of the Blessed Virgin Mary.

Seventy-five years earlier, little Jacinta Marto of Fatima told everyone who would listen to her that peace in the world has been entrusted to Mary, the Mother of Jesus Christ. Jesus told Fatima visionary Lucia that the world must know

Six tons of Russian Bibles, rosaries and scapulars were brought to Russia by the Peace Pilgrims.

Coronation of the Pilgrim Statue of Our Lady of Fatima at midnight in Red Square in front of armed militia.

Father John Hoke, who had been leading the Rosary lifted up a small statue to be used for the coronation. A small crown from the infant Jesus of Prague statue was used. The pilgrims believe that Jesus Christ personally wishes His Mother to be honored as Queen of All Mankind.

Bishop Paul Hnilica, was consecrated Bishop 40 years earlier behind the Iron Curtain. His diocese symbolically extended from Peking to Moscow. He wept openly as the statue was crowned and said: "At this moment we see Mary's triumph complete. There is no more communism. There is no Soviet Union. We acknowledge her Queenship with this coronation.

One pilgrim claims to have seen immense flashes of light over Red Square during the coronation. In the light, the pilgrim saw the Blessed Virgin Mary dressed as Our Lady of Fatima, holding a large Rosary and wearing a radiant crown. Rays of light streamed from her hands down into the square and then up and out in all directions.

Father Henry Bordeaux, OCD was present and the pilgrim is known to him. He signed this statement:

"As confessor to the person who reported this vision I can testify that the said person has all the signs of authenticity: holiness, humility, obedience and soundness of mind with no trace of hysteria. Based on my personal knowledge of the person and the circumstance, it is credible that Our Lady appeared in Red Square in the manner described."
(Photo taken by anonymous pilgrim.)

Pilgrims bring the Icons of Jesus King of All Nations and Our Lady of Guadalupe (also known as Our Lady of The Americas) to the place at Red Square where the great Cathedral of Our Lady of Kazan was demolished in 1917 by the atheist regime.

Holiness is an absolute attachment to the will of God which strives always for union with Him through grace. 5 It implies detachment from sin and evil. Through Jesus, who is the only-begotten both of His Heavenly Father and His human Mother Mary, we become children of God.

As Pope Pius X said in AD DIEM ILLUM "Furthermore, the most Holy Mother of God had not only the honor of having given the substance of her flesh to the only-begotten Son of God, who was to be born of the human race (St. Bede)....

but she was also entrusted with the task of tending and nourishing this victim and even of offering It on the altar at the appointed time. The result was a never-broken community of life and labor between Son and Mother..."

The underlying theme of all the Marian apparitions is the call of our Blessed Mother to each person on earth to join her in the way of life she lived on earth: love, consecration, penance and reparation. The penance involves a daily mortification of personal willfulness in order to perform God's will heroically

with great love of daily duty. The reparation she specifically desires involves a message given at Fatima: "Many nations will be annihilated..." To prevent this annihilation, the Blessed Mother specifically stated, "I shall come to ask for the consecration of Russia to my Immaculate Heart and the Holy Communion of Reparation on the First Saturday of each month." 6

Attached to her fourfold request for Love, Consecration, Penance and Reparation is a special promise from the Mother of God:

I promise to assist at the hour of death with graces necessary for salvation, all those who, on the first Saturday of five consecutive months receive Holy Communion, recite a part of my rosary and keep me company for fifteen minutes while meditating on the fifteen mysteries of the rosary, with the intention of making reparation to me. 7

An Act of Consecration to Jesus through Mary that is used by The Holy Father, Pope John Paul II is the Saint Louis de Montfort prayer:

In the presence of all the heavenly court I choose thee this day for my Mother and mistress. I deliver and consecrate to thee, as thy slave, my body and soul, my goods, both interior and exterior, and even the value of all my good actions, past, present and future; leaving to thee the entire and full right of disposing of me, and all that belongs to me, without exception, according to thy good pleasure, for the greater glory of God in time and eternity.

Pilgrims on the Peace Flight of Thanksgiving to Russia believe that Jesus wants the world to honor the Immaculate Heart of His Mother along side devotion to His own Sacred Heart. Responding to this belief, the pilgrims, escorting the Pilgrim Statue of Our Lady of Fatima risked everything to honor Mary as the Victorious Queen of the World on this historic journey.

Lucia said the exact words of Jesus were:

I desire devotion to My Mother's Immaculate Heart to be placed along side devotion to My Own Sacred Heart. 8

Pope Pius XII referring to the Pilgrim Statue of Our Lady of Fatima said:

"It is the Queen of Angels herself who goes forth from this Sanctuary of Fatima where Heaven permitted us to crown her Queen of the World..... to make jubilee visits to all her dominions."

Miracles and healings have occurred wherever the Pilgrim Statue is given hospitality. The Holy Father said "... miracles of grace are multiplied in such a way that we can hardly believe what we see taking place." Those who pray before the Pilgrim Statue notice that as the intensity of prayer deepens the statue changes in appearance. Cardinal Tedeschini, the Pope's Legate to the ceremonies of Fatima for the closing of the Holy Year in 1950, claimed that when the Pilgrim Statue was in Rome, the Pope had seen a reenactment of the "miracle of the sun" over the Vatican. 9

30

Gammeil art from the Basilica of Lourdes

Pray for the Light to comprehend who
Jesus Christ is.

PART II

The Pilgrim's Prepare

Before I come as the just Judge, I am coming first as the King of Mercy. Before the day of justice arrives, there will be given to people a sign in the heavens of this sort:
All lights in the heavens will be extinguished, and there will be great darkness over the whole earth. Then the sign of the cross will be seen in the sky, and from the openings where the hands and the feet of the Savior were nailed will come forth great lights which will light up the earth for a period of time. This will take place shortly before the last day.

Words of Jesus Christ to Blessed Sister Faustina

Poland, 1934

AN ACT OF CONSECRATION
TO OUR LADY OF THE MIRACULOUS MEDAL

O Virgin Mother of God,
Mary Immaculate,
we dedicate and consecrate ourselves
to you under the title of
Our Lady of the Miraculous Medal.
May this Medal be for each one of us
a sure sign of your affection for us
and a constant reminder of our duties toward you.
Ever while wearing it,
may we be blessed by your loving protection
and preserved in the grace of your son.
O most powerful Virgin, Mother of our Savior,
keep us close to you every moment of our lives.
Obtain for us, your children,
the grace of a happy death;
so that, in union with you,
we enjoy the bliss of heaven forever. Amen.
O Mary, conceived without sin,
Pray for us who have recourse to you. (3 times.)

NOVENA PRAYER

O Immaculate Virgin Mary, Mother or Our Lord Jesus and our Mother, penetrated with the most lively confidence in your all-powerful and never-failing intercession, manifested so often through the Miraculous Medal, we your loving and trustful children implore you to obtain for us the graces and favors we ask during this Novena, if they be beneficial to our immortal souls, and the souls for whom we pray. (Here privately form your petitions.) You know, O Mary, how often our souls have been the sanctuaries of your Son who hates iniquity. Obtain for us then a deep hatred of sin and that purity of heart which will attach us to God alone so that our every thought, word and deed may tend to His greater glory. Obtain for us also a spirit of prayer and self-denial that we may recover by penance what we have lost by sin and at length attain to that blessed abode where you are Queen of angels and of men. Amen.

CHAPTER III

Paris

*Paris is considered by many
Marian scholars to be the repository
of great graces from heaven
for a sinful world.*

Ru Du Bac Chapel where Saint Catherine Laboure met the Blessed Mother and later received visions of the Miraculous Medal. The miraculous incorrupt body of Saint Catherine Laboure rests in this chapel on the right under the statue of Our Lady Queen of The World.

OUR LADY OF THE MIRACULOUS MEDAL

Paris was the first stop for the pilgrims. Known as the City of Lights, Paris is considered by many Marian scholars to be the repository of great graces from heaven for a sinful world. A seat of intellectual giants, the arts, literature, industry and geopolitics have flourished in the city that is sometimes referred to as "sin city."

Great turmoil came to Paris during the French Revolution when the innocent and the guilty alike watered the earth with their blood. On July 18, 1830, four days after Bastille Day when the French celebrate their freedom from corrupt, autocratic monarchy, the Mother of Jesus Christ came to call upon a young postulant at 140 Rue du Bac, in the Chapel of the Motherhouse of the Sisters of Charity.

Young Catherine Laboure was awakened from sleep by a little angel who tapped her shoulder and said "Catherine come quickly. The Blessed Virgin is waiting for you in the Chapel". Shocked, filled with awe and frightened too, young Catherine said to the angel, "If I get out of my bed to go to the Chapel, I will awaken the others". The angel insisted. "Hurry, the Blessed Virgin is waiting." Quickly dressing, Catherine accompanied the angel. She wasn't certain that her feet ever touched the ground as she rushed through the convent to the Chapel, whispering all the while, "Glory be to the Father and to the Son and to the Holy Spirit". With the little angel at her side she entered the Chapel. It was ablaze with light. Falling prostrate before the Blessed Sacrament, Catherine experienced the exquisite awareness of the Real Presence of Jesus in the Eucharist hidden behind the tiny doors of the tabernacle. The little angel was also prostrate before the tabernacle. "He sees the face of God," Catherine realized. "My Lord and My God", she murmured as she swooned in the ecstasy of mystical union. In that moment a human tastes a drop of divinity. Never again do created things satisfy.

The little angel summoned the young postulant and directed her gaze toward a chair upon the altar. The light was almost blinding as it enveloped the Blessed Virgin Mary who was seated there. Like a lost child who finally finds her mother, Catherine leapt to her feet and raced to the Blessed Virgin Mother. Falling to her knees, she laid her head in the lap of the Mother of God and wept with abandon.

Catherine Laboure was clinging to her Eternal Mother as she cried out "Dear Mother, I have looked for you everywhere. I have called to you day and night. Dearest Mother, never leave me again." Catherine gazed at the beautiful face of the Blessed Virgin Mary, an icon of tenderness, as she heard these words:

I have always been with you my child.

I never leave any of my children. I am always with each of you.

The Mother of God, drying Catherine's tears, humbly asked her if she would undertake a mission on behalf of the children of God.

The times are evil. Great darkness has entered into the heart of mankind. Do not be afraid. The Lord loves you very much. He loves all His children. For that reason He has sent me to you with this assignment. If you accept you must faithfully give the messages I confide to you to this unbelieving world. You will be contradicted. You will have much suffering but you will have the grace to bear everything. Much will happen in your lifetime. Misfortunes will fall upon France. The kingdom will fall. The Church will be severely prosecuted. Evil will spread to the whole world as the spirit of rebellion is unleashed.

At those words Catherine shuddered.

Holding both Catherine's hands, the Blessed Mother continued.

Those children of God who come to their brother, Jesus, especially in the Blessed Sacrament, will receive great graces. Remember my beloved Catherine, I am your Eternal Mother.

I am always with you. I am with all my children. You can always find me when you come before the Blessed Sacrament. Where Jesus is I am too.

At those words, Catherine "forgot" the presence of the Blessed Virgin Mary. Her heart was once again lost in the Real Presence of Jesus in the Blessed Sacrament.

As the weeks turned into months Catherine tried to look for the Blessed Mother every time she entered the Chapel. But something unexplainable had happened to her that extraordinary night. Now, when Catherine Laboure came near the Blessed Sacrament, a wound, so deep that no consolation could salve, drove her deeper and deeper into prayer that cries out for mystical union: Jesus. Only Jesus. Her prayer was answered, for Catherine was now often in that world where Jesus and she were one.

Catherine was kneeling in the Chapel with all the other nuns the second time she saw the Blessed Virgin Mary. Suddenly, to the right of the tabernacle, Catherine saw the Blessed Mother standing upon a globe bathed in a mysterious light so bright that she seemed "clothed in the sun."(Rev.:12)

The Blessed Mother was exquisitely dressed in resplendent robes as the Queen of Heaven and Earth. There were three rings on each of her fingers. As the Blessed Mother opened the palms of her hands, great rays of light shone from them upon the globe. Catherine then heard these words in her heart,

The ball which you see represents the planet Earth. These rays which shine from my hands symbolize the graces God has entrusted to me to give to those children of His who ask me for them. The gems from which rays do not shine are the graces for which my children forget to ask.

The vision was more intense now. Catherine saw the rays from the Blessed Mother's hands defuse immense light upon all parts of the globe. Then an unusual, golden, oval door formed around the vision of the Blessed Mother. There were words around the door frame which Catherine Laboure could see and as she read these words, they were emblazoned upon her heart.

**Oh Mary, conceived without sin,
Pray for us
Who have recourse to you.**

Then the young postulant had another locution. 1

My beloved daughter, Catherine, please have a medal made to represent the vision God has allowed you to see. All those who wear this medal around their neck with confidence will have great graces.

What Catherine had seen was the front of what would come to be called the miraculous medal.

Then the vision changed. The Blessed Mother faded into the immense light that had accompanied her visual presence. Catherine strained to look into the light. She saw the outline of a large M appear. A bar went through the M and then a cross shone forth in the middle. Catherine was amazed as she began to see two hearts under the M. One was encircled with thorns; the other was pierced by a knife. Twelve stars surrounded this vision in the oval door. As Catherine gazed at the vision, she understood the two hearts to represent the Sacred Heart of Jesus and the Immaculate Heart of Mary. What Catherine was seeing was the back of the miraculous medal.

Catherine Laboure told no one of her visitation with the Mother of God, or of her vision and locution, except her confessor. She led the life of a humble servant, in obscurity, as a nun at 140 Rue du Bac, until her death. Many years later she was canonized by the Universal Church. Today her body rests in the very chapel where her visions and locutions for the world occurred. Her incorrupt body rests in a glass casket under a side altar. People come from all over the world to view this ongoing miracle.

Many today believe God sent the Blessed Virgin Mary to Saint Catherine Laboure to remind mankind of His plan for the salvation of all. The Immaculate Conception of Mary, in the womb of her mother Anne, presumed the Incarnation of the Second Person of the Holy Trinity. The creation of Mary is a pure gift to mankind from the Trinity. In Mary, God carved out an exception to the consequences of the sin of Adam and Eve. "I will send the woman and her seed will destroy the seed of the evil one." (Genesis 3:15). Mary is that woman.

Conceived without original sin, Mary was created so that the Word of God, Jesus, could come to mankind through a sinless mother. Without her sinlessness, Jesus would have died of loneliness. The relationship between Jesus and Mary, out of which the children of Adam once again become children of God, demonstrates on a human level, that reciprocity of love which is the relationship of the Three Persons of the Holy Trinity. Jesus is both God and man. It is from the Eternal Father, through Jesus, that all children of God receive their divinity. It is from Mary, through Jesus, that all children of God receive their redeemed humanity.

Through the Incarnation of Jesus, God restored His people of the earth to the place He intended from the beginning: His children and heirs to the kingdom of heaven. As evil proliferates on the planet earth, the Eternal Father sends the Eternal Mother, Mary, Mother of Jesus, to remind His beloved children of His plan for their return to Paradise, which is life with Him.

The priest who counselled Catherine Laboure, aware of the reason for apparitions of the Blessed Virgin, was wise and faithful. He protected the anonymity of this favored Sister of Charity. Through his courage, he cooperated with Divine Providence to have the Miraculous Medal produced and distributed to the world. Devotion to Mary under her title of the Immaculate Conception spread to the entire world. Twenty five years later, the Catholic Church, under Pope Pius IX, promulgated the dogma of the Immaculate Conception on December 8, 1854. The medal that depicts this dogma has come to be known universally as the Miraculous Medal because so many miracles and blessings have been reported by the faithful from all over the world who wear it.

37

The Chapel at Rue Du Bac

The incorrupt body of Saint Catherine Laboure, an on going miracle, rests in the glass casket on the side altar below the statue of Our Lady Queen of the World.

Father Edgardo M. Arellano, affectionately known as Father Bing speaks to the Peace Pilgrims about miracles and the value of penance.

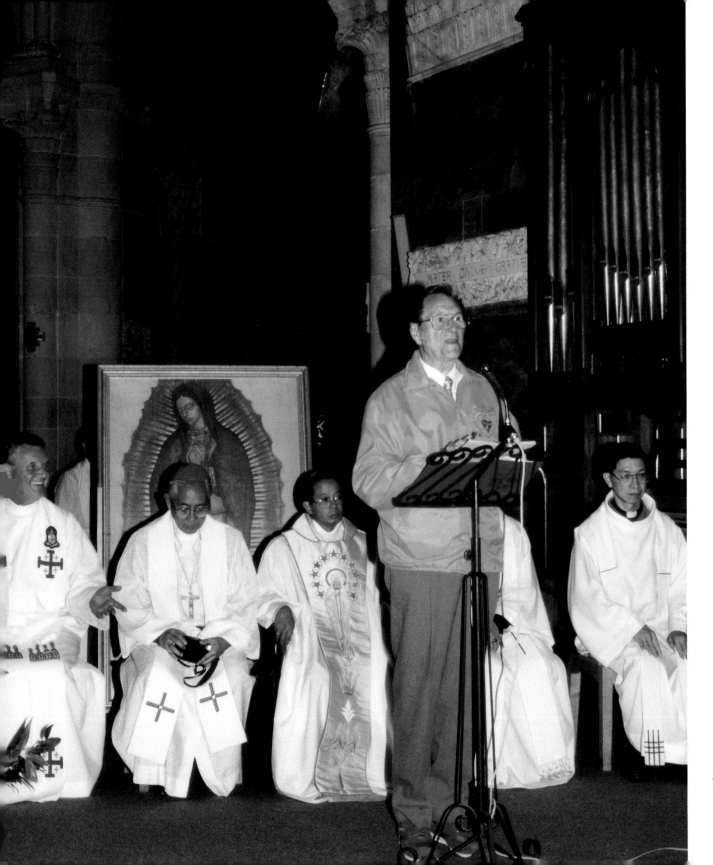

THE ANGEL'S PRAYER

*Most Holy Trinity, Father,
Son and Holy Spirit,
I adore Thee profoundly.
I offer Thee the
Most Precious Body,
Blood, Soul and Divinity
of Jesus Christ,
present in all the tabernacles
of the world, in reparation for
all the outrages, sacrileges and
indifference by which
He is offended.
And through the infinite merits
of His Most Sacred Heart, and
the Immaculate Heart of Mary,
I beg of Thee the conversion
of poor sinners.*

John Haffert, founder of The Blue Army of Our Lady of Fatima, addresses Peace Pilgrims in Paris.

Our Lady of Victories

Around the corner from the convent of St. Catherine Laboure is Our Lady of Victories Church in Paris. During the French Revolution, 1789, it was closed as a church. Some forty years later, when the church was reopened, it was difficult to obtain a church-going congregation. One day the Pastor had a locution 1 as he said Mass:

Consecrate the parish to the Most Holy and Immaculate Heart of Mary.

The Pastor made a public announcement of his locution. To his amazement 400 people attended the consecration that night.

A century later France was at war. Many thought all was lost. In the church of Our Lady of Victories on January 17, 1870 the people were praying to the Sacred Heart of Jesus and the Immaculate Heart of Mary. The priest leading the prayers heard by locution:

"This day, between eight and nine o'clock France has been saved by Our Lady of Victories' intercession." 2

The pastor immediately declared:

"So that all future generations shall know that at this hour France was saved by Our Lady of Victories we shall place here a Silver Heart in honor of the Immaculate Heart of Mary. Tomorrow we will begin a Novena of Thanksgiving." The Armistice was signed the day the Novena of Thanksgiving ended. 3 Jesus has promised that those who trust Him are never disappointed. The Fatima visionaries, nearly fifty years later, would learn from Jesus Himself that He has entrusted peace in the world to the Immaculate Heart of His Mother 4

In another part of France, at that very hour, a great apparition of Our Lady occurred in the village of Pontmain. The message Our Lady gave as the villagers prayed the rosary was;

"Pray my children. My Son permits Himself to be touched by your prayers."

Some years later, in the church of Our Lady of Victories, a Novena was said for a dying child, Therese Martin from nearby Alencon. At the conclusion of the Novena, a statue on the bedside table of little Therese became alive and smiled at her. Later, Therese's widowed father brought her to visit the Church of Our Lady of Victories. In her writings, Saint Therese of Lisieux recalled her pilgrimage of Thanksgiving. "What I felt in her Sanctuary (in Our Lady Victories Church) I cannot say. The graces she granted me resembled those of my First Communion. I was filled with peace and joy. It was there that my Mother, the Virgin Mary, told me distinctly that it was indeed she who cured me". 5

MEMORARE

Remember, O most compassionate Virgin Mary, that never was it known that anyone who fled to your protection, implored your assistance, or sought your intercession, was left unaided. Inspired with this confidence, we fly unto you, O Virgin of Virgins, our Mother; to you we come; before you we kneel sinful and sorrowful. O Mother of the Word Incarnate, despise not our petitions, but in your mercy hear and answer them. Amen

39

The Fifteen Promises of Mary to Those Who Recite the Rosary

1. *Whoever shall faithfully serve me by the recitation of the Rosary, shall receive signal graces.*
2. *I promise my special protection and the greatest graces to all those who shall recite the Rosary.*
3. *The Rosary shall be a powerful armour against Hell; it will destroy vice, decrease sin, and defeat heresies.*
4. *It will cause virtue and good works to flourish; it will obtain for souls the abundant mercy of God; it will withdraw the hearts of men from the love of the world and its vanities, and will lift them to the desire of eternal things. Oh, that souls would sanctify themselves by this means.*
5. *The soul which recommends itself to me by the recitation of the Rosary, shall not perish.*
6. *Whoever shall recite the Rosary devoutly, applying himself to the consideration of its sacred mysteries shall never be conquered by misfortune. God will not chastise him in His justice, he shall not perish by an unprovided death; if he be just he shall remain in the grace of God, and become worthy of eternal life.*
7. *Whoever shall have a true devotion for the Rosary shall not die without the sacraments of the Church.*
8. *Those who are faithful to recite the Rosary shall have, during their life and at their death, the light of God and the plentitude of His graces; at the moment of death they shall participate in the merits of the Saints in Paradise.*
9. *I shall deliver from Purgatory those who have been devoted to the Rosary.*
10. *The faithful children of the Rosary shall merit a high degree of glory in Heaven.*
11. *You shall obtain all you ask of me by the recitation of the Rosary.*
12. *All those who propagate the Holy Rosary shall be aided by me in their necessities.*
13. *I have obtained from my Divine Son that all the advocates of the Rosary shall have for intercessors the entire Celestial Court during their life and at the hour of death.*
14. *All who recite the Rosary are my children, and brothers and sisters of my Divine son Jesus Christ.*
15. *Devotion of my Rosary is a great sign of predestination.*

(Given to St. Dominic and Blessed Alan) Imprimatur:
Patrick J. Hayes, D.D., Archbishop of New York

CHAPTER IV

Lourdes

*Faith alone discloses the ultimate
meaning of life.*

Mary the Mother of God,
Gamaeil Art at Lourdes Basilica depicting the first apparition of the
Blessed Virgin Mary to Saint Bernadette.

Statue of Saint Bernadette at Lourdes

Trouble continued to brew in France. Widespread unemployment, disease and moral breakdown were everywhere. No class was exempt. High in the Pyrenees was a town known as Lourdes. Four years after the dogma of the Immaculate Conception was promulgated, eighteen visions were seen by a sickly, emaciated young girl of eleven. The daughter of a sometimes employed father, ill with alcoholism, and a mother who was forced to compensate for her husband's considerable shortcomings, Saint Bernadette Souberous was perceived by many as an unlikely prospect for favors from heaven. Her family was not respectable. Bernadette had no outward indication of piety. In fact, she was so uneducated that she had not been able to learn her catechism. It was understandable that, at first, few believed her story of visions of a Beautiful Lady in the grotto. God alone knows the scorn the child suffered for her faithfulness to the Beautiful Lady from Heaven who imparted three secrets to Bernadette.

One day the pastor of the town asked Bernadette to inquire, during her vision, the identity of the Beautiful Lady. Credibility comes in strange circumstances. The shivering child stood knocking at the pastor's door as the rain and wind bit at her thin frame. Finally the priest opened the door. "Oh, it's you again," he snapped. "Don't you realize I'm busy? I have work to do," he mocked.

Bernadette was terrified as she sputtered, "The Beautiful Lady said, "I come from Heaven. I am the Immaculate Conception." Stunned, the priest awoke. Half choking, half weeping, he said, "Please come in... Can you ever forgive me?"

Miraculous waters gushed forth from the site of the apparition. Obedient little Bernadette responded to the Beautiful Lady's request for penance and humiliations to unmask the terrible spirit of pride and rebellion in the world. Kneeling, Bernadette dug in the mud of the grotto and even ate some of the mud. "She's insane," some onlookers hooted. "What do you expect?", others scorned. But as the child dug deeper into the mud, a bubbling sound was heard. Then a trickle came out of the mud. Soon all could see a stream. Gradually, the sick began to come to these waters of Lourdes. For over one hundred and fifty years, the sick and the well have come from all over the world to bathe in the miraculous waters given by the Beautiful Lady at Lourdes, even in these times.

And Bernadette? She spent her short life in a convent at nearby Nevers

43

Procession of the sick (les invalides) at Lourdes as the Holy Eucharist is carried for healing and blessing.

Grotto at the actual site of the apparitions of the Blessed Virgin Mary to Saint Bernadette at Lourdes.

Each year millions from all over the world, of all faiths, come to Lourdes to experience healing, Spiritual renewal, to obtain Divine favors, or to express thanksgiving to God. Extraordinary healings and favors occur in the miraculous waters of Lourdes, especially in these times

where today, visitors may see her incorrupt body miraculously preserved for more than 100 years. It rests encased in glass under the main altar. The Beautiful Lady had told her, "I don't promise you happiness in this life, but in the next."

Bernadette's sacrifice, however, brought blessings to her family. Her father was given some respect because of the eighteen miraculous visions of his daughter. He found meaningful employment and spent his old age somewhat awed at his role in the apparitions. As for Bernadette's mother, one can only conjecture that as her husband's self-image and financial capacity improved, so also the family shared in the goodness of God's mercy.

The message from Lourdes was once again the gospel message: love, consecration, prayer and sacrifice are the path to Paradise. It is love, prayer and sacrifice that free the world from darkness, from blindness to God's presence in the world. God is the PERFECT SERVANT. He serves ALL. Each person on earth is called by God to be a servant too, with Him. Prayer is life with and in God. Those who do not pray are unable to love. They are lost children. They live in torment. For them Paradise is unknown.

Midnight candle procession at Lourdes.

Prayer

(Composed by St. Therese of Lisieux)

Jesus, Who in thy bitter Passion
didst become "the reproach of men,
and the Man of Sorrows"
I venerate Thy Holy Face
on which shone the beauty
and gentleness of Divinity.
In those disfigured features
I recognize Thine infinite love,
and I long to love Thee
and to make Thee loved...

May I behold
Thy Glorious Face in Heaven!

46

CHAPTER V

Lisieux

She promised to spend her eternity showering roses of favors upon the earth to God's children.

The Basilica of Saint Theresa of the Child Jesus at Lisieux. The largest Church in the world built to honor any Saint (except Saint Peters in Rome).

The statue of Saint Therese of Lisieux surrounded by petitions of pilgrims.

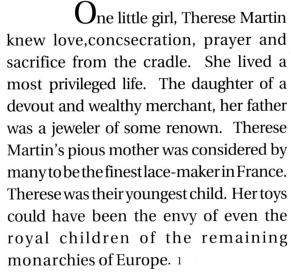

One little girl, Therese Martin knew love, concsecration, prayer and sacrifice from the cradle. She lived a most privileged life. The daughter of a devout and wealthy merchant, her father was a jeweler of some renown. Therese Martin's pious mother was considered by many to be the finest lace-maker in France. Therese was their youngest child. Her toys could have been the envy of even the royal children of the remaining monarchies of Europe. 1

Therese had indomitable confidence in the Merciful Heart of Jesus from earliest childhood. One day she heard of a violent murderer who rapaciously killed not only his mistress, but also his mistress' young daughter. Sentenced to die by the guillotine, the condemned murderer refused to repent and receive the Sacraments of the Church. Little Therese told her family that she was praying and doing sacrifices out of love for this man. Therese told her family she <u>knew</u> the murderer would be converted for "Jesus is so merciful!"

The murderer was known to have a heart of stone. Therese prayed constantly. She did little acts of mortification. Three days were remaining before the execution. Therese slept without her pillow. The

murderer cursed the priest the next day. That night Therese slept on the floor. The following day the criminal continued to curse God. Therese discarded her coverlet as she again slept on the cold floor, pleading with Jesus through the night to change the murderer's heart. All were amazed the next day for, as the guillotine was readied, the condemned criminal cried out for a crucifix. His last words were of sorrow for his crime and trust in the mercy of Jesus. Therese only said, "I knew it. Jesus is Mercy!" Her family never forgot. They, and the rest of the world learned much from little Therese.

That child is known today as St. Therese of Lisieux. As a tiny girl she experienced mystical union while playing in the garden of her home. A fire of such intense love for God was ignited in her little heart that no allure of the world, no creature, not even her beloved parents and sisters could fill the longing she felt for God alone. Her soul developed as a confidant of the Child Jesus, who was her playmate, her beloved, her source (in the Trinitarian sense) and her goal. She had an exquisite understanding of Jesus as Mercy.

49

Statue of The Child Jesus in the Basilica of St. Therese of Lisieux. Saint Therese knew the Child Jesus as a playmate and confidant.

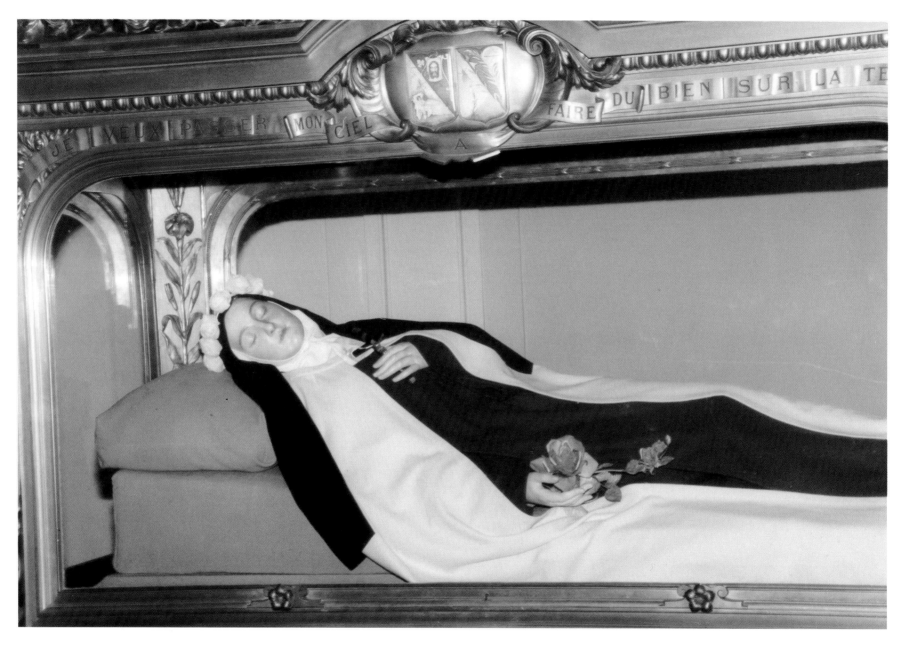

Wax depiction of Saint Therese of Lisieux.

Therese journeyed to Rome to gain the approval of the Pope to enter the Carmelite Convent at Lisieux at age 15. There, as the bride of Christ, she lived her "little way." Her motto was, "All for the love of You, dear Jesus." Therese died at the age of 23. Her spiritual journal found its way to the whole world. The diary of Saint Therese is a masterpiece of divine union lived out one day at a time in that human obscurity where God and Therese were one. The "little way" is a sure path to Paradise.

The Church of Saint Therese built at Lisieux may be the largest in the world dedicated to a saint. After her death, Therese became known throughout the world as the Little Flower of the Child Jesus. She had promised to spend her eternity showering roses of favors upon the earth to God's children. Some say the miracles given by God through Saint Therese of Lisieux are the most prolific of any saint. Her "little way" to Paradise is practiced all over the world in these times.

51

Actual photo of Saint Therese of Lisieux.

" The era of the Holy Spirit is the era of peace achieved by celebrating the alliance of the two hearts through the communion of reparation"

PLEDGE TO LIVE THE COMMUNION OF REPARATION

O Victorious Queen and Mother of the World,
in imitation of your holy spouse, St. Joseph.
I totally consecrate my heart to be one
with yours., that it may be one
with the Heart of Jesus.
I pledge to live the Communion of Reparation
everyday of my life, by meditating
on the mysteries of the rosary,
by wearing the scapular as a sign
of my union and consecration,
by reconciling my heart through the
daily examination of conscience, by frequently
going to confession, by receiving Our Lord in the
Eucharist in Holy Mass and by making
the Holy Hour in reparation for the outrages and
blasphemies committed against your
Immaculate Heart and the Sacred Heart of
your Son, Our Lord Jesus.
I solemnly promise to help organize this
communion of reparation in my parish,
in close coordination with my pastor and bishop,
every first Friday and Saturday of each month.
O dearest Mother, please send forth the graces
of the Flame of love to all mankind
so that the Era of Peace
which you so promised may come. Amen

52

CHAPTER VI

Fatima

A Mother's Prayer

53

May all my children love one another.

PEACE PLAN FROM HEAVEN
Given by Our Lady
AT FATIMA

1. Pray the Rosary.
2. Personal consecration professed by wearing the scapular.
3. Penance through sanctification of daily duty with recommended fasting on Wednesdays and Fridays.
4. Renewal of the consecration of the world to the Immaculate Heart of Mary.
5. Promote and honor the Alliance of the Two Hearts by the First Friday and First Saturday Communions of Reparation.

Courtesy of the
Blue Army of
Our Lady of Fatima

The dove in flight was seen in the sky over the Shrine on the 75th Anniversary of the Apparition. (note faint hint of Rainbow.)

THE FIRST APPARITION AT FATIMA

There were seven apparitions of the Blessed Virgin Mary at Fatima, and there were seven messages for the world. The first occurred on Sunday, May 13, 1917. Ten year old Lucia, eight yeay old Francesco and seven year old Jacinta were playing in the bucolic hills of Portugal. Suddenly great flashes of light frightened them and they jumped to their feet to quickly gather the sheep. At that moment Lucia and Jacinta saw a Beautiful Lady in the light who was "more brilliant than the sun." She spoke to them but only Lucia heard:

> *Fear not, I will not harm you.*
> *I am from Heaven.*

Lucia summoning all her courage asked: "What do you want?" The Beautiful Lady from Heaven said:

> *I ask you to come here for six consecutive months, on the 13th day, at this same hour. I will tell you later who I am and why I have come to you. I shall return here again a seventh time.*

Lucia timidly asked, "Dear Beautiful Lady, may I go with you to Heaven?

55

The Great Shrine of Fatima on the 75th Anniversary of the apparitions of the Blessed Virgin Mary in 1917.

Procession after Mass returning the original statue to the Cova - the exact place Mary first appeared.

for the conversion of sinners?

The three little children responded: "We will do as you ask."

The Blessed Virgin Mary then opened her hands and great streams of light radiated upon the children. Lucia later spoke about that moment:

"This light penetrated us to the very depths of our heart, and allowed us to see ourselves in God, Who was that Light more clearly than we see ourselves in a mirror. Then we were moved by an inner impulse, also communicated to us, to fall on our knees, while repeating:

Most Holy Trinity
I adore you .
My God My God
I Love You in the
Most Blessed Sacrament.

The parting message of the Blessed Virgin Mary to the children was:

Say the Rosary everyday to earn peace for the world and the end of war. (World War I)

Little Jacinta, describing the conclusion of the fateful apparition said: "When she went back to heaven the doors seemed to shut so quickly that I thought her feet would get caught." 1

And Jacinta and Francesco too?"

The Beautiful Lady responded:

You all will come to Heaven with me. Francesco must pray many rosaries.

Francesco, at this time, could only see the miraculous light, but he could hear Lucia speaking to a presence in the light. The Beautiful Lady said to Lucia,

Let him pray the Rosary.. In that

way he too will be able to see me.

Francesco immediately began to pray his Rosary. After one decade he saw the Mother of God! It was then that the Beautiful Lady said:

Do you want to offer yourselves to God, to endure all the sufferings He may choose to send you as an act of reparation for the sins by which He is offended and as a supplication

THE SECOND APPARITION

The second apparition at Fatima occurred on June 13, 1917. Perhaps only fifty people were present when the Beautiful Lady from Heaven once again appeared in that glorious, mystical light that always envelopes "the woman clothed with the sun" (Rev.12). On that warm, beautiful day the Blessed Virgin Mary taught the three children this prayer to add to each decade of the rosary:

Oh my Jesus, forgive us our sins,
Save us from the fires of hell,
Lead all souls to heaven,
Especially those most in need of Thy mercy.

The Mother of God then made a special request of Lucia. She asked her to learn to read! In those times, in that rural village, such a request for a girl to learn to read was indeed considered radical. The Blessed Mother also told Jacinta and Francesco that she would take them to heaven soon. But for Lucia, the Blessed Mother said:

You will remain on the earth for a long time. My Son Jesus wants to use your life to make me known and loved. He wants to establish devotion to my Immaculate Heart in the world. 2

57

The Famous Miraculous Consecrated Host of Santarem is held up for veneration. It is of flesh and bleeds. It is appoximately 300 years old. It is one of the great Spiritual treasures of Portugal and of the entire world.

Then the Mother of God made a promise on behalf of her Divine Son:

I promise salvation to those who embrace devotion to my Immaculate Heart.

Their souls will be loved by God as flowers placed by me to adorn His throne. These souls will suffer a great deal but I will never leave them. My Immaculate Heart will be their refuge, the way that will lead them to God.

Lucia's third Memoir describes the scene: "She opened her hands and pierced our hearts with the light that streamed from her palms. It seems then that the first purpose of this light was to give us a special knowledge of a special love for the Immaculate Heart of Mary just as on two other occasions it gave us a knowledge of God and the mystery of the Holy Trinity. From that day on we felt in our hearts a deeper love for the Immaculate Heart of Mary."

THE THIRD APPARITION

By July 13, 1917 thousands of people made their way to the village of Fatima and to the cove near the oak tree above which the apparition had occurred in the two preceding months.

A fine, cool breeze was blowing, even though it was the height of summer. The people were silent. Suddenly, there was a bussing sound and people noticed a small cloud moving in above the oak tree where it hovered.

The three children then saw the Mother of God in the mystical light. She said:

I want you to come back here on the 13th of next month. Continue to say the Rosary every day in honor of the title God has given me, Our Lady of the Rosary, to obtain the peace of the world, the end of the war, because in these times, only under that title can the peace be obtained. You children must come here every month and in October I will tell you who I am and what I want. I will then perform a miracle so that all may believe.

The Mother of Jesus Christ, at that moment, made an appointment between time and eternity. She spoke of a divinely obtained cosmic miracle that all might believe.

Then the Beautiful Lady asked:

Sacrifice yourselves for sinners. Say often, especially when you make some sacrifice: **My Jesus it is for love of You, for the conversion of sinners and in reparation for sins committed against the Immaculate Heart of Mary.**

Then the Beautiful Lady opened her hands. Profound and immense light poured from her palms and appeared to penetrate the earth. Lucia in her Memoir recounts: "Our Lady showed us a large sea of fire which seemed to be beneath the earth. Plunged in this fire were the demons and the souls who were like embers, transparent and black or bronze colored, with human forms which floated about in the conflagration, borne by the flames which issued from it with clouds of smoke, falling on all sides as sparks fall in great conflagrations, without weight or equilibrium, among shrieks and groans of sorrow and despair, which horrified us and caused us to quake with fear. The devils were distinguished by horrible and loathsome forms of animals, frightful and unknown, but transparent and blank. This vision vanished in a moment. Providentially, our good heavenly Mother had promised us in the first apparition to take us to heaven. Otherwise, I think we would have died of fright and horror." [3]

"In the July 13th vision of hell, the children, by special illumination saw self-love, undisguised and naked, consuming

itself from within. They heard every jealousy, pride, greed, lust and the assorted choir of all the vices, shouting and shrieking and screaming in the disharmony and harshness of their own intimate natures. They saw the final state of those called to love who make a final, unchangeable choice not to love. They saw the disorder of sin, undisguised by its usual trappings, as it is in its essence." [4]

History demonstrates that few responded to this message from Heaven of 13 July 1917. The "unknown light" promised as a sign preceeding World War II occurred on January 25-26, 1938. The international newspapers referred to it as an "Aurora Borealis." A youth in Ireland was an eyewitness of the strange light. He said it was such an ominous and mystical light that it knocked him off his bicycle. As he lay in the dust he promised the Lord he would become a priest should God spare him whatever punishment that ominous light portended. He did become a priest. Only years later did he learn of Fatima and Our Lady's message of the "unknown light." He scoffed, "An Aurora Borealis! Oh the pride of men. How it blinds us all to truth." That priest, now a well-known Monsignor, works tirelessly to spread the messages of Our Lady. He says "Ireland alone could have prevented World War II. The problem is, we didn't know about Fatima in time!" [5]

The great secret given to the children in 1917 at Fatima is that peace and the Immaculate Heart of Mary are very much intertwined in God's plans for mankind. [6] Little Jacinta, who died soon thereafter, began to speak of war as hell on earth. "She was conscious of hell as representing God's justice and the Immaculate Heart of Mary as representing His mercy." [7] Among her final words were:

59

Famous painting of The Two Hearts in Rome.

"Oh if I could only put into everybody's heart the burning fire I have inside me which makes me love the hearts of Jesus and Mary so much! The Heart of Jesus wishes to be honored together with the Immaculate Heart because God has entrusted peace to her. [8]

THE FOURTH APPARITION

By 13 August the crowd grew to nearly 15,000 people. This time there were no visionaries for they were in jail. Once again the little cloud was seen to hover over the oak tree in the Cova de Iria in Fatima. There were explosion sounds and a trembling like an earthquake. Then came the mystical light. An eyewitness said: "As we walked around... our faces were reflecting all the colors of the rainbow - pinks, reds and blues... The trees suddenly seemed to be made not of leaves but of flowers. The ground reflected these many colors and so did the clothes we wore." [9]

The crowd became angry that the children had been kidnaped and imprisoned by local officials.

THE FIFTH APPARITION

It was 19 August and the visionaries were back in their village. Our Lady came to Fatima that day to the area of Valinhos. She said:

Come again to the Cova de Iria on the 13th of next month and continue to say the rosary each day. In October I will perform a miracle so that everyone can believe in the apparitions. If they (the officials) had not taken you to the town (prison) the miracle would be even greater. Saint Joseph will come with the Holy Child to bring peace to the world. Our Lord will come to bless the people. Our Lady of the Rosary and Our Lady of Sorrows will also come at that time.

The Mother of God asked for a children's procession. She asked that two litters be made to carry donations from pilgrims. The Blessed Virgin specified that she wished Lucia and Jacinta and two other girls dressed in white to carry one litter. Francesco with three other boys, dressed in white robes, were to carry the other in the procession. She asked that the donations be used to celebrate the feast of Our Lady of the Rosary. The Blessed Virgin promised that some of the sick would be healed. She pleaded:

Pray , pray a great deal, and make sacrifices for sinners, for many go to Hell for not having someone to pray and make sacrifices for them.

The children of Fatima never recovered from the awesome awareness Our Lady gave the world with those parting words of her August apparition. She asked her faithful children to become prayer warriors on behalf of all people on earth. The gates of Hell will stay closed if the Blessed Mother's children take her August 13, 1917 message to heart. If many go to Hell because no one prays and makes sacrifices for them, then as prayers and sacrifices increase in these times, as thinking people become aware of Divine truths, the number of lost souls will decrease proportionately to the level of spiritual awareness.

Saint Joseph, who has always been considered by Christians as the patron of happy deaths, was named in the August apparition. Tradition has held that Saint Joseph, heretofore hidden in Scripture and often in devotion would emerge as a powerful figure in the last times. The Blessed Virgin promised that he would come to Fatima with the Christ Child to bring peace to the world.

For many, by the twilight of the twentieth century, family life is a memory. It is a source of great tension for others. Few enjoy peaceful, joy-filled family relationships. Does the Holy Family of Nazareth, under the leadership of St. Joseph, play a roll in the restoration of family life? Does the secret of world peace depend on family life?

Painting of death of Saint Joseph in St. Peters Basilica, Rome.

of penance. Such knowledge is a Divine grace. Only those who pray understand penance. The materialist has no appreciation of penance which is sacrificial love. Penance does not involve deriving pleasure from pain in the form of sadism. Penance, self-sacrifice flow from love.

An eyewitness of the 13 September apparition, Monsignor Quaresma, Vicar-General of the diocese said in his journal:

"At midday there was complete silence. One only heard the murmurs of prayers. Suddenly there were sounds of jubilation and voices praising the Blessed Virgin. Arms were raised pointing to something in the sky. "Look, don't you see? Yes, yes, I do... There had not been a cloud in the deep blue of the sky, and I too raised my eyes and scrutinized it in case I should be able to distinguish what the others, more fortunate than I, had already claimed to have seen. With great astonishment I saw, clearly and distinctly, a luminous globe, which moved from the east to the west, gliding slowly and majestically through space. My friend also looked, and had the good fortune to enjoy the same unexpected and delightful vision. Suddenly the globe, with its extraordinary light disappeared. Near us was a little girl dressed like Lucia and more or less the same age. She continued to cry our happily: "I still see it. I still see it! Now its

THE SIXTH APPARITION

The crowds grew by 13 September, 1917. Estimates were that the number had swelled to perhaps 30,000 people. By now the behavior of the visionaries left little doubt in their neighborhood that their apparitions were from a Divine source. The children were so markedly different than before the messages from Heaven that few questioned the Divine grace with which they were blessed. The visionaries sought out solitude to pray. Play time became prayer time. Prayer was their only pleasure. They began to wear a heavy rope under their garments because, not only was it uncomfortable, it actually caused pain that they could offer to Jesus for the conversion of sinners. Their memory of Hell was so acute that suffering became a blessing because the Beautiful Lady had taught them the value

coming down...!"

Monsignor Quaresma was later heard to say: "That globe I saw was Our Lady!" [10]

Those near Lucia heard her ask: "Dear Beautiful Lady what do you want of me?" Although Francesco enjoyed the privilege of seeing the Beautiful Lady, he could not hear her words. Only Lucia and Jacinta saw and heard the Beautiful Lady respond:

> *Let the people continue to say the Rosary every day to obtain the end of war. In the last month, in October, I shall perform a miracle so that all may believe in my apparitions. If they had not taken you to the town to prison the miracle would have been greater. St. Joseph will come with the Baby Jesus to give peace to the world. Our Lord will also come to bless the people. Besides, Our Lady of the Rosary and Our Lady of Sorrows will come.* [11]

The Seventh Apparition

By October 13, the press was aware of the promised cosmic miracle. The O Dia of Lisbon carries this description: "For days prior to the thirteenth, groups of pilgrims traveled toward Fatima. They came on foot, buskins on their brawny legs, food bags on their heads, across the pine groves where the windmills rotate. A slow and swaying gate swung the hems of their skirts from side to side and waved orange kerchiefs upon which sat their black hats...People from everywhere whom the voice of the miracle had reached, left their homes and fields, and came on foot, by horse or by carriage. They traveled the highways and the roads, between hills and pine groves. For two days these came to life with the rolling of carriages, the trot of the donkeys and the voices of the pilgrims...Water dripped from the caps and broad-rimmed hats onto the new jackets of their suits for seeing God. The bare feet of the women and the hobnailed shoes of the men sloshed in the wide pools of the muddy roads. They seemed not to notice the rain... A murmur drifting down from the hills reached us. It was a murmur like the distant voice of the sea lowered faintly before the silence of the fields. It was the religious songs, now becoming clear, intoned by thousands of voices. Over the plateau, over a hill, or filling a valley, they were a wide and shuffling mass of thousands upon thousands of souls in prayer." [12]

Great flashes of light signaled the beginning of the final apparition of Fatima.

Lucia, besieged by the crowds, asked the Beautiful Lady about cures for the sick who were present in large numbers. The response was:

It is necessary that they amend their lives and ask pardon for their sins. Some will be cured and others will not.

Lucia describes the apparition in her fourth Memoir:

"Her face became grave as she continued: 'Let them offend Our Lord no more, for He is already much offended.' And opening her hands she made the light emerging from them ascend to where the sun ought to be. And while it was arising, her own radiance continued shining towards the sun."

Saint Joseph appeared in the sky. It was the moment for the great cosmic miracle of the sun. This miracle was seen, not only by the seventy thousand people in the Cova de Iria, but it was also seen by people within a radius of at least thirty miles. The poet, Alfonso Lopes Vieira, working at noon on the veranda of his home, thirty miles away, in San Pedro de Muel, saw the phenomenon and in surprise called for his wife and her mother to come and see. At Alburitel, nine miles from Fatima, the school teacher, Senhora Delfina Pereira Lopes, ran with the children into the street. There, others prayed and shouted and cried, thinking the world was coming to an end. The Baron of Alvaiazere, an attorney of Ourem, had come to the Cova for diversion. He was braced against the force of collective suggestion. He later wrote: "I knew it was necessary to be on my guard, not to allow myself to be influenced. I only know that I shouted, "I believe, I believe, I believe, I believe" and that tears fell from my eyes, wondering, ecstatic before this manifestation of divine power." [13]

Lucia wrote in her Memoir about the miracle of the sun:

"Here you have, Your Excellency, the reason why I shouted that they should look at the sun. My purpose was not to bring attention of the crowd to the sun, because I didn't notice them. I was not even aware of their presence. I did so, moved by an inner force which impelled me to act thus. When Our Lady disappeared in the immense distance of the sky, next to the sun we saw Saint Joseph holding the Child Jesus and Our Lady dressed in white with a blue mantle. Saint Joseph and the Child seemed to be blessing the world, making the sign of the

The icon of the Fatima apparitions held by Dr. Rosalie Turton.

cross. Shortly after this vision had vanished, I saw Our Lord and Our Lady who reminded me of Our Lady of Sorrows. Our Lord was blessing the world as was Saint Joseph. This vision vanished too, and it seemed to me I again saw Our Lady in a form resembling that of Our Lady of Mount Carmel." 14

The visionaries later told the people Saint Joseph and the Child Jesus were both dressed in red, while Our Lady wore a white dress with a blue mantle, which is her attire as Our Lady of the Holy Rosary. 15

Saint Joseph came with the Child Jesus to "bring peace to the world." Is God's will for the world manifested in the Holy Family? Mary appeared with Joseph and Jesus attired as Our Lady of the Rosary. Her constant message to the world has been to pray the Rosary. Saint Joseph's part in bringing peace also is connected with the rosary. 16 "In the way of Divine Providence, the achievement of this (peace) needs the help of Saint Joseph, not only as intercessor, but as model for husbands and fathers. The love of Joseph for the Immaculate Heart, her love for him, their mutual love for the Child all combine to throw light on the dynamics that bring peace." 17

One terrible warning given by the Blessed Mother at Fatima has not yet been fulfilled. "Several ENTIRE NATIONS will be ANNIHILATED." Today mankind has the means of annihilating the planet.

In 1925, the Blessed Virgin appeared once again to Lucia in reference to the July 13, 1917 message of Fatima. This time she brought the Christ Child with her. The apparition happened in Pontevedra, Spain in a convent where Lucia was a postulant. It was on this occasion that the First Saturday Devotion of Reparation to the Immaculate Heart was requested of the entire world.

In 1929, the Blessed Virgin again appeared to Lucia to announce the time for the consecration of Russia to her Immaculate Heart. Lucia, by then a nun, communicated this request to her confessor, her Bishop, and the Holy Father. The Portuguese Bishops did consecrate Portugal to her Immaculate Heart. Portugal was spared any involvement whatsoever in World War II. It was not until October 31, 1942 that Pope Pius XII consecrated the universal church and the world to the Immaculate Heart of Mary. World War II was raging. It took three years to conclude consequences in motion at that moment of consecration. The Second World War ended in 1945. Pope Paul VI renewed the consecration of the world to the Immaculate Heart of Mary in 1964 at the second Vatican Council.

Once more he publicly made the consecration at Fatima during a pilgrimage celebrating the 50th anniversary of the apparitions of the Mother of God to the three children.

Lucia communicated to church authorities that a proper consecration of the world to the Immaculate Heart of Mary occurred only in October 1984 when Pope John Paul II acted in concert with the Bishops of the world. She cited as her source for that statement, the Lord Jesus Christ.

The Blessed Mother yet again gave a warning to her children in 1973 at Akita, Japan on the actual anniversary of her great cosmic miracle at Fatima. The presiding Bishop has stated that he believes this message is the Third Secret of Fatima, given once again for the world.

If my children do not respent and better themselves the Father will allow a terrible punishment upon them. All humanity will be involved. It will be a punishment greater than the deluge. Fire will fall from the sky and will wipe out a great part of humanity. The living will envy the dead... I alone can still save you from the calamities that approach. [18]

The apparitions at Akita were the first apparitions to be approved by the Universal Church in more than fifty years.

The Lord Jesus Christ told Sister Lucy, the sole living visionary of Fatima in March 1939:

Ask, ask insistently for the promulgation of the Communion of Reparation on the first Saturday of each month. The time is coming when the reign of My justice will punish various nations. Some of them will be annihilated. [19]

God's justice is not like man's justice. God has no cruelty. God's justice cleanses. When mankind sins he blinds himself to God's love and tranquility and order. As man withdraws from God's protection he succumbs to the work of evil spirits infesting the planet earth. God, in His infinite love, has allowed man the freedom to choose good. A person who does not pray, a person who does not fast is helpless to distinguish between good and evil. In the 20th century as prayer and fasting decreased, mankind's spiritual blindness increased to the point that the planet upon which all people on earth dwell may be in mortal danger of extinction.

Amazingly, most people on earth are unaware of this.

But the Blessed Virgin calls herself the Queen of Peace in these times. She says we are on the path of peace. [20]

The three little shepherds

65

Solid silver art form depiction
The Eternal Father holding the "key" to heaven
in the Cathedral of Prague.

PART III

The Pilgrims Triumph

67

I will put enmity between you and the woman, and between your offspring and hers: he will strike at your head while you strike at his heel.

(Gen. 3:15)

To The Miraculous Infant of Prague

Dearest Jesus, Little Infant of Prague, how tenderly You love us!
Your greatest joy is to dwell among men and to bestow Your blessing upon us.
Though I am not worthy that You should behold me, I feel drawn to You by love
because You are kind and merciful, and because You exercise almighty power over me.
So many who turn to You with confidence have received graces
and had their petitions granted. Behold me as I kneel before You and lay open my heart to you
with its prayers and hopes. I present to You especially this request, which I enclose in Your loving Heart:
(Mention your request)
Rule over me, dear Infant Jesus, and do with me and mine according to Your holy Will,
for I know that in Your Divine wisdom and love You will arrange everything for the best.
Do not withdraw Your hand from me, but protect and bless me forever.
I pray You, all-powerful and gracious Infant Jesus, for the sake of Your Sacred Infancy,
in the name of Your Blessed Mother Mary who cared for You with such tenderness,
and by the greatest reverence with which Saint Joseph carried You in his arms,
help me in my needs. Make me truly happy with You,
sweetest Infant, in time and in eternity, and I shall
thank you forever with all my heart.
Amen

Almighty and Everlasting God, Lord of heaven and earth, who revealed Yourself to little ones,
grant, we beg You, that we who venerate with due honor the sacred mysteries of Your Son, the Child Jesus, and imitate His example,
may enter the Kingdom of Heaven which You have promised to little children. Through the same Christ Our Lord. Amen

CHAPTER VII

Prague

*The more you honor Me the more
I shall bless you.*

This is the original Statue of The Infant Jesus of Prague
which is in the church of Saint Alphonse in Rome
in these times.

Bishop Bacani thanks the congregation in the Cathedral of Prague.

The Soviet controlled government of Czechoslovakia was not able to extinguish the faith of the people during its reign of oppression in last half of the 20TH Century. Cardinal Tomasek said, "We bear the cross, but in the cross there is light, and in the light there is victory... Our Lady is the sign of victory." 1 How well he articulated the promise of the Eternal Father to all mankind in Genesis 3:15.

I will put enmity between you (Satan) and the woman, (Mary) and between your offspring and hers: He will strike at your head while you strike at his heel.

The people of Czechoslovakia maintained a heroic devotion to Our Lady of Fatima and the Fatima promises throughout the long, atheistic occupation.

Prague is renown as the city that housed the famous Infant Jesus of Prague Statue. This special devotion to the Infant Jesus began in the early 17TH Century in Bohemia.

Princess Polyxenia of Labkowitz received a statue of the Divine Child, previously brought from Spain, as a wedding present from her mother. After her husband's death, the princess devoted herself to works of charity and was noted for her assistance to the Carmelites in Prague. By 1628 the Carmelite monastery was in a state of financial discord. The princess donated all of her material possessions to the Carmelites, including her mother's wedding gift with this prophecy: "I give you what I prize most highly in the world; honor and respect

Peace Pilgrim, Tom Collins reads scripture in the Cathedral of Prague.

Pilgrims join the congregation of worship
in the Cathedral of Prague.

the Child Jesus and you shall never be in want." Her words are as valuable today as they were in those times. The statue of the Infant Jesus was placed in the Oratory of the convent. Carmelite Father Cyril had a locution as he prayed before the statue in 1635.

"Have mercy on Me and I will have mercy on you. Return My hands to Me and I shall give you peace. The more you honor Me the more I shall bless you." Father Cyril noticed that both hands of the statue were missing. After repairing the statue, peace and prosperity were restored to the Carmelites. 2 Devotion to the Infant Jesus has always been practiced by the Carmelites for it is through their Mother, the Blessed Virgin, that the Divine Child came into the world. Devotion to the Lord Jesus Christ as the Infant Jesus of Prague has spread to the entire world. This devotion is a powerful recognition of the awesome humility of God.

ACT OF CONSECRATION TO THE HOLY SPIRIT

On my knees before the great
multitude of heavenly witnesses
I offer myself, soul and body to You,
Eternal Spirit of God.
I adore the brightness of Your purity
the unerring keeness of Your justice and the
might of Your love. You are the Strength and Light of
my soul. In you I live and move and am.
I desire never to grieve You by unfaithfulness
to grace and I pray with all my heart to be
kept from the smallest sin against You.
Mercifully guard my every thought and grant that I
may always watch for Your light and listen to Your
voice and follow Your gracious inspirations.
I cling to You and give myself to You and ask
You by Your compassion to watch over me in my
weakness. Holding the pierced Feet of Jesus
and looking at His Five Wounds and trusting in
His Precious Blood and adoring His opened Side and
stricken Heart I implore You Adorable Spirit Helper
of my infirmity, so to keep me in Your grace
that I may never sin against You.
Give me grace O Holy Spirit,
Spirit of the Father and the Son
to say to You always and everywhere
"Speak Lord for Your servent heareth."
Amen

CHAPTER VIII

Russia

*Once again the invisible God
has shown His people that faith cannot
be proved by visible signs.*

Peace Pilgrims at Red Square in Moscow on the 75th Anniversary of the destruction of the Basilica of Our Lady of Kazan.

Freeing the Icon from the ruins, people were astounded at the "presence" they experienced in the Holy Image of the Mother of God and her Divine Son. Almost immediately many miracles occurred for those who venerated the Icon. It has come to be known as the "Liberatrix" and Protectress of Holy Mother Russia.

In 1917 the Bolsheviks saw the Icon of Our Lady of Kazan as an expression of the "soul of the Russian people." They therefore destroyed the Basilica of Our Lady of Kazan at Red Square. By this act, the Soviet government intended to prove to the people that God does not exist. Officials boasted that they were able to destroy the Basilica of the Liberatrix and Protectress of Holy Mother Russia. What they did not know was that as they destroyed the Basilica of Our Lady of Kazan at Red Square, in another place in Europe, the Mother of God was appearing to three shepherd children in the village of Fatima, Portugal.[2] She spoke to them about atheistic Russia:

Russia will spread her errors and terrors world wide. In the end my Immaculate Heart will triumph. Russia will be converted.

Once again the invisible God has shown His people that faith cannot be proved by visible signs. Faith is grounded in belief in the Word of God and the tra-

On October 16, 1917, Polish Saint Maximillian Kolbe (who at that time had never heard of the apparitions and messages of the Blessed Virgin Mary at Fatima) said:

"One day the cavaliers of Our Lady will carry her statue over the Kremlin to the heart of Moscow."[1]

In the burned out ruins of a monastery in Russia the Icon of Our Lady of Kazan was discovered because of an apparition of the Blessed Virgin Mary.

Kazan lies deep in the heart of the former Mongolian Empire. The Blessed Mother appeared to a small, eight year old girl in Kazan one day and told her the whereabouts of the Icon in the ruins of the old monastery.

Our Lady of Kazan Icon
The Patroness and Protectress of ALL Russia

This is the sacred and revered Our Lady of Kazan Icon which
miraculously was removed from Russia at the time of the Bolshevic
Revolution. It was discovered in a castle in England later in this
century. Today it is housed in a beautiful shrine at Fatima, Portugal.

ditions of His Church.

According to Marian Theologian Theophane Carroll, writing in <u>The Virgin Mary in the Separated Eastern Churches,</u> "There is almost perfect agreement between the Orthodox Church and the Catholic Church in regard to Marian doctrine and devotion to Our Lady... In the east (Orthodox Church), there has never been a re-look at Mary. What was taught about her from the beginning is taught today, and there is an uninterrupted stream of tradition coming from the apostles to the present day... The doctrine which the western Fathers taught was the same doctrine that the eastern Fathers taught. What was believed in the east, was also believed in the west."

Seventy five years after the destruction of the Basilica of Our Lady of Kazan at Red Square, the Peace Pilgrims arrived in Moscow on the Russian feast of Our Lady of Victories. It is also called the feast of Our Lady of Intercession and it commemorates a great victory of the Russian people over Tartar invaders.

The Patriarch of Moscow and of all Russia, his Holiness Aleksy II received

God's Love brings Peace to mankind.

Moscow Cathedral

One thousand years of schism died silently in the crucible of love, prayer, and sacrifice at Moscow Cathedral as the Archbishop prayed with Father Ken Roberts and the two congregations. The Peace pilgrims and the Orthodox parish together responded Amen.

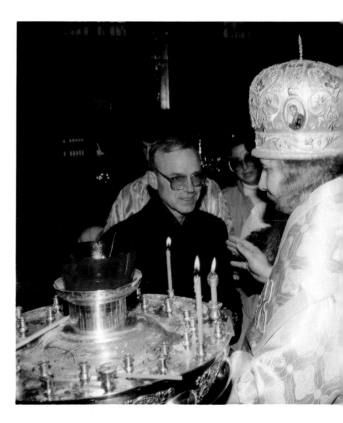

a delegation of the Peace Pilgrims led by Father Ken Roberts of the United States. [3] The Patriarch's main concern was the motive behind the Peace Pilgrims. "Are they (the Pilgrims) holy?" he inquired of the cavaliers of Our Lady. [4]

The Russian Orthodox Archbishop told the entire congregation in Moscow Cathedral: "We know of the message of Fatima. During the dark years that message was our hope. We know that the original Icon of Our Lady of Kazan is in Fatima. We look forward to its return to Russia. We have a miraculous copy here at which people have come to pray. Let us together pray before it."

The Archbishop continued: "Those who have kept the faith should not be proud. Acknowledge that we are all sinners. Now we have a great task to accomplish."[5]

Father Ken Roberts presented an Icon of Fatima to the Archbishop who responded,"I accept this in the name of His Holiness, the Patriarch of all Russia." [6]

The Icon of Fatima
presented by Father Ken Roberts to the Archbishop of Moscow,

THE CHAPLET OF UNITY

Jesus told His servant; *"pray this Chaplet of Unity under My Sovereign Kingship."*

The Chaplet is recited on ordinary rosary beads. Groups may divide the recitation between Leader (L) and Responders (R). If you are alone recite both parts. Recite on the large bead before each of five decades:

L - God our Heavenly Father, through Your Son Jesus, our Victim-High Priest, True Prophet, and Sovereign King, Pour forth the Power of Your Holy Spirit Upon us and Open our Hearts.

R - In Your Great Mercy, through the Motherly Mediation of the Blessed Virgin Mary, our Queen, forgive our Sinfulness, Heal our Brokenness, and Renew our Hearts in the Faith, and Peace, and Love, and Joy of Your Kingdom, that we may be One in You.

Recite on the ten small beads of each of five decades

L - In Your Great Mercy, Forgive our Sinfulness, Heal our Brokenness, and Renew our Hearts.

R - That we may be One in You.

Conclude in unison with:

**Hear, O Isreal! The Lord Our God is One God!
O Jesus, King of All Nations, May Your Reign Be
Recognized On Earth!
Mary, Our Mother and Mediatrix of All Graces, Pray
and Intercede For Us Your Children!.
St. Michael, Great Prince and Guardian of Your
People, Come With The Holy Angels and Saints and
Protect Us!**

Archbishop of Moscow, Father Gerald McGinety of Ireland and Father Ken Roberts of the United States of America.

THE CHAPLET OF THE DIVINE MERCY

The Lord said to sister Faustina (1905-1938):
You will recite this chaplet on the beads of the Rosary in the following manner:

First of all you will say one Our Father, one Hail Mary, and one Apostles' Creed. Then, on the Our Father Beads say these words:

"Eternal Father, I offer Thee the Body and Blood, Soul and Divinity of Thy Most Beloved Son and our Lord and Savior Jesus Christ, in atonement for our sins and the sins of the whole world."

On the Hail Mary Beads say the following words:

For the sake of His Sorrowful Passion have mercy on us and the whole world.

In conclusion say Three Times these words:

Holy God, Holy Mighty One, Holy Immortal One, have mercy on us and on the whole world.

Three O'Clock in the afternoon - The Hour of Great Mercy

At three o'clock implore My mercy especially for sinners; and, if but for a brief moment, steep yourself in My Passion, particularly in My abandonment at the moment of agony. This is the hour of great mercy for the whole world. ... In this hour I will refuse nothing to the soul that makes a request of Me in virtue of My Passion.

CHAPTER IX

Poland

*Sow happiness about you
because you have received
much from God.*

The Ancient and Revered Black Madonna Icon in the
Shrine of Our Lady of Czestochowa.

Copy of the famous Black Madonna,
Our Lady of Czestochowa,
resides in Basilica of St. Maximillan Kolbe in Poland

On the mountain of Jasna Gora overlooking the city of Czestochowa, Poland, stands the Shrine of Our Lady of Czestochowa. Contained in the Shrine is the ancient and greatly venerated "Black Madonna".

Legend has it that St. Luke the evangelist painted a picture of Our Lady with the Christ Child on a piece of cypress wood cut from the table of the Last Supper. In the 4th Century, Saint Helen, Mother of Constantine the Great, obtained this treasure. In 1338 a great Shrine was built to house this painting of the Virgin and Child by St. Luke in the Jasna Gora. Abundant graces and favors have come to those who have prayed before this sacred painting. [1]

In 1430 some self-styled crusaders who did not believe in the Real Presence in the Eucharist plundered many holy shrines in Europe. Among these was the sanctuary of the Black Madonna. Though the painting has been exquisitely restored, the saber cuts in the face of the image of Our Lady could not be repaired.

The Blessed Virgin Mary has been proclaimed Queen of Poland and the entire nation has been placed under her protection. The Shrine of Our Lady of Czestoshowa is considered by many as one of the holiest places in the world. [2]

Many pilgrims claim Poland was the spiritual highpoint of the journey.

Shortly before the Pontificate of Pope John Paul II, members of Our Lady of Fatima Blue Army attempted to take the Pilgrim Statue to Warsaw. Officials of the Russian atheist regime refused to allow the statue off the plane. Father Matthew Strumski made a wire outline of the Blessed Mother out of coat hangers to be carried to the places where the Pilgrim Statue was intended.

The Polish people were outraged. How dare any official forbid the Blessed Virgin Mary Pilgrim Statue entrance to their land, they demanded. Prime Minister Gierek went to Cardinal Wyzinski personally to invite the Pilgrim Statue of Our Lady of Fatima into Poland. It was too late. The Fatima group with the Pilgrim Statue had already departed. Public opinion was near the boiling point. [3]

The Cardinal, seizing the opportunity, obtained permission from the Prime Minister to build eight new churches. (Twenty four churches had been destroyed during the war.)

On August 22, 1979, the Feast of the Queenship of Mary, the Blue Army

Maryanne King a Peace Pilgrim, explains this photo:

"In 1946 the Fatima youth conference conceived the idea of the Pilgrim Virgin Statue that would someday go to Russia. Poland was one of the very early countries that wanted it to come and in 1946 it was taken there, but a Russian general refused to allow it off the airplane. The common people were furious and a wire silhouette of the statue was made and taken to the churches instead. The anger of the people was so great that the general realized he made a tactical error and called the cardinal to apologize and ask that the statue be brought back. Being rather shrewd, the cardinal got a concession before he'd ask to have the statue again! Many churches were destroyed or damaged in the war and he got permission to build a new one. It was built mostly with money from American-Polish people and completed in a year. In the back of that church is the silhouette of the Fatima Statue. The night of the Mass at the cathedral one of the American Polish priests asked to speak and he told the people in Polish the story and finished by saying that a Russian general had refused entry to the Fatima Statue that had come to Poland from Fatima. This priest had been there when the Statue was refused entry. Many of the Polish people were in tears that night and perhaps that is why they were so open and receptive to us. We did not hear the story until later, but the love of the people was very moving. The statue was in Worsaw for almost three days and visited both cathedrals. The people held all night vigils and when it travelled on they accompanied it to the airport with hymns, music, and festive costumes. This greatly astonished the airport guides who seemed alert and nervous but it delighted all the participants!"

83

returned to Poland with the Pilgrim Statue of Our Lady of Fatima.

Cardinal Wysznski gave the blessing in the newly constructed church of Our Lady Queen of the World as the Pilgrim Virgin Statue was carried in procession. Finally it was placed beside the wire outline which had been carried through Poland as a sign of love, prayer and sacrifice. 4

Shortly thereafter His Eminence Karol Cardinal Wojtyla of Poland became Pope John Paul II.

Helen Kowalska was born near Warsaw on the birthday of the Blessed Mother, August 5, 1905, one year before Lucia of Fatima. On 22 February, 1931, Helen, now known as Sister Mary Faustina of the Blessed Sacrament, was a member of the Congregation of Our Lady of Mercy in Poland. That day she saw a vision of the Lord Jesus Christ who told her to paint an image of Him duplicating the vision. In those times, many geo-politicians believed that a second World War was impossible. Several years later, the Lord Jesus once again appeared to Sister Faustina in a vision. Pale and red rays enveloped the entire surroundings and then spread out over the entire world. This vision has been memorialized in the

The Knights of Columbus at Our Lady of Victory Church in Poland.

His Holy Priests
are His Hands.

His Holy Priests
are His Heart.

image which is universally recognized as the Divine Mercy.5

At the end of her young life, Sister Faustina received the Holy Eucharist from an angel. Her one occupation was to live in the presence of God, Our Heavenly Father. She died at the age of 33 and was Beatified in Rome on Divine Mercy Sunday, April 18, 1993 by her countryman Pope John Paul II.

The following is a message she lived:

Act in such a way that all those who come n contact with you come away joyful. Sow happiness about you because you have received much from God; give, then, generously to others. They should take leave of you with their hearts filled with joy even if they have no more than touched the hem of your garment. 6

Divine Mercy Painting
in St. Maximillan Kolbe Church

Rome

This is my Holy City

*The Peace Pilgrims finished their journey in Rome at the Vatican
where they participated in the canonization ceremonies of the Spanish Martyrs.*

St. Petersburg
Cathedral of Our Lady of Kazan built by Peter the Great
where a replica of the Icon of Our Lady of Kazahoused.
The atheistic government of the Soviet Regime turned this
Cathedral into an office building

CHAPTER X
The World

All people throughout the world, whether they know it or not, engage daily in the battle between goodness and evil, darkness and light. Russia, with over three hundred different ethnic groups and nationalities may be the ransom for peace in the world as the people of the vast former Soviet Empire begin the arduous pilgrimage from repression to freedom. Those who study the messages of the Blessed Virgin Mary given to the world at Fatima and at her other approved apparitions enjoy a deep sense of trust in the role the Blessed Virgin has and will play as all people struggle toward peace.

Those who pray much realize that solutions have little lasting effect or value unless they flow from the will of God. Those who pray much experience a deep resonance of spirit with the messages of the Blessed Virgin Mary at her approved apparitions as she calls for peace through commitment to truth regardless of the cost.

Though there will be hard times as the Twentieth Century draws to a close, **there will be incredible victories as good triumphs over evil.** Those who consecrate, or

entrust their lives to the care of the Mother of Jesus Christ trust that she stands next to them in their prayers before the throne of God. The saving grace for mankind in these times flows from the Immaculate Heart of Mary and the Sacred Heart of her Divine Son. Their heavenly joy has grown out the depths of suffering from the darkness of the cross to the light of the Resurrection.

The world groans toward the light of peace. Jesus' very entrance into humanity was heralded with God's promise of peace to those of good will. Peace must reign in the silence of mankind's heart. Only then will peace reign in the world. Peace in the world is the fruit of peace in mankind's heart. Peace is the child of forgiveness. Forgiveness is the child of love. Love is only possible through prayer. Prayer is the echo of mankind's longing calling to God's Heart.

The culmination of all the approved apparitions of the Blessed Virgin in modern times is the fulfillment of her requests and promises, especially as articulated at Fatima. No approved apparition however, is more important than another. Each brings the same Mother of God who, by Divine Edict is

the Mother also of all people. Since she is the most humble of all God's creatures, the Blessed Mother never interferes in any life unless she is invited.

Each person on the earth today has a role to play in the unfolding of the great Plan God has for His beloved children to live in peace, joy and love. Each person has received the gift from God of freedom, to choose good or evil; darkness or light; God's will or not.

In these times, many people of all races, nationalities, faiths and beliefs see miraculous and unexplained healings from physical and emotional impairments. People also claim to see the miracle of the sun. Many rosary beads have in fact changed color from silver to gold. Hidden beneath all these signs is the Triumph of the Immaculate Heart.

The world teeters on the brink of self-destruction in the waning hours of the Twentieth Century as it labors into the early stages of the Triumph of the Immaculate Heart. Those who love seem to carry immense sorrows. But amidst the turmoil, the great song of the Angelic Court that was heard by the shepherds on that first Christmas Eve is once again entering into the sweet silence of mankind's heart as the Queen of the Angels is manifested on a global scale. Her presumed presence is the longing of all mankind for universal peace, love and joy. Her call is the Good News of the Gospel of Jesus Christ.

Hurry and be converted a loving Mother tells a sleeping world. She is forming the Light of the Sacred Heart of Jesus.

The remnant flock hears the words: PEACE ON EARTH TO PEOPLE OF GOOD WILL - GOD'S WILL. Out of the great purification that mankind begins ,even now, to experience, will come not only personal renewal, but also renewal of the universal church.

Our Lady grieves over lack of respect for Jesus in the Eucharist. God's children are called to make reparation for this attitude and behavior. The Eucharist is Real Food. The Eucharist is Jesus. Jesus is God. Those who eat Jesus' Body and drink Jesus' Blood never die. Jesus is the Bread of Life. Jesus is the Nourishment for Life in God. God sustains. Mankind chooses. The Evil One works tirelessly to discredit belief in the Real Presence of Jesus in the Eucharist and intellectually attacks Mary as the Mother of the Church, and the Holy Father as the appointee of Christ to lead the church on earth.

The pilgrim people of God keep Jesus in their hearts. They live only for Him. All else passes away. They stay hidden in His Heart for His Heart is a crucible where He prepares them for life with our Father. His Heart is mankind's home on earth. Focused on the Gospel, the pilgrim people of God serve Our Lady faithfully when they "...Do whatever He (Jesus) tells (them)". (John 2:1-11) They are surrendered to His ways. They live only the life He showed all people, for all times, when He too walked the earth as we do now. Any other path but His takes the pilgrim people of God far away from the Kingdom of our Father and His waiting arms. Life on earth is short. Those who live His life on earth are a light to the world.

Satan never sleeps. He diverts, distorts, trying to destroy. He is the father of lies. The Blessed Virgin Mary is the gift of God the Father Who has given her the task from all eternity of overcoming Satan and his wiles. She is the hope of mankind in the battle of darkness and light. When humanity had forfeited Paradise, the Eternal Father in His great love for His poor, lost children made a promise. "I will send the Woman (Mary). Her seed (Jesus and His followers) will crush the head of the serpent (Satan). (Gen. 3:15).

The Soviets did not know about the apparitions of the Blessed Virgin Mary at Fatima. The books containing the messages of Our Lady at Fatima were the most dangerous books in the Soviet Empire to Satan's plans for the holy people of Russia. Satan fears the messages of the Blessed Mother of Jesus Christ. Her love and humility crush his invidious program of hatred, greed, war, violence, poverty, sickness and death. Her Divine Son is the Savior of the World. She is the perfect imitator of His Virtue. Those who would follow her Divine Son are like her. Those who love hear her admonitions.

War is a punishment for sins. War among men would cease if God's children would pray and fast. The war today is with the unseen world. The battle for souls is fierce. The weapons of victory are prayer and fasting.

Jesus loves His Mother's Rosary. It is His life on earth. When people walk with Jesus on the path of His life on earth, they learn how to follow Him to Paradise. Do you see why the Rosary is the chain that binds those who pray it to His ways, His will, His Life? He asks all to come to Him with the chain of eternal life, the Rosary, in their hands and in their heart.

God's world is a rich playground for His children. Soon there will be no evil hearts left on His playground. Though His children weep in their suffering today, by His love, by His ways, they shall laugh as they play before His face tomorrow.

The Triumph of the Immaculate Heart is a mission beyond human capability. It is a Divine Plan. These are the times of Satan's greatest battle against the church, against the beautiful children of God. Pope Paul VI, in his Encyclical Letter SIGNA MAGNA, spoke about the apocalyptic battle between Woman and the Dragon. He said: "These are those apocalyptic times." The warnings of Scripture awaken the spirit to truth. "We are not contending against flesh and blood, but against the powers against the world rulers of this present darkness, against the spiritual hosts of wickedness in the heavenly places." (Eph. 6:12)

Mary, the Woman of Genesis 3:15, is the Great Sign of God's deep, unfathomable love for each child of His on this planet. It is through Her Immaculate body, with her consent, that He chose to dwell among mankind as man. Pope Pius XII reminded the war-weary world: The son of Mary, "...the man Jesus Christ is also the Son of God and God Himself"! Mary is the Mother of life in God. Those who do not live in God die. Mary stands at the threshold of death. She protects her own. It is God's will that the world be consecrated to her Immaculate Heart.

God has created and chosen each person on this planet to live these apocalyptic times of the most important battle in history. The opportunity exists for more saints than at any other time since the begining. Could it be that Canonization will come for entire groups, like the Spanish Martrys? God never loses.

Mary, the Mother of all the people of God is giving birth to a new age on His planet. Their Son Jesus has redeemed His people.

Now Jesus shall reign as Lord and Master and Ruler.

God's Earth shall be clean.

God's earth shall be pure.

God's people shall sing and dance before His Face

As they love one another.

The wedding feast of the Lamb comes.

God's children are shedding their garments of sin and self-love.

They will make merry in garments whiter than fresh-fallen snow.

They shall wear garments washed in the Blood of the Lamb.

God's highly favored daughter Mary is here for all His children.

She brings Jesus to each child of His.

She gives Jesus to each child of His.

Each of His children shall hold His dear Son Jesus.

Hands defiled with greed, averice, sloth have no strength to hold Jesus.

Hearts filled with lust and anger have no love to welcome Jesus.

Intellects filled with pride have no wisdom to comprehend Jesus.

It is Mary who prepares God's children

To celebrate well at the Wedding Feast of the Lamb.

God is restoring His Kingdom on earth.

Such is The Triumph of The Immaculate Heart.

A mosaic of the last apparition of Fatima to Lucia.

Epilogue

The Eternal Father

ROME

This is My Holy City.

I have sent you here to My Voice.

You, in your obedience, shall bring great joy to My sleeping children.

How they shall sing and make merry as they return to the Ancient City of My Voice.

The very stones rise up and greet you, My little ones.

Be at peace for you have followed My Heart to this Holy City.

Your joy shall not diminish.

I am the Ancient One, My Children.

My Holy City rises up like incense before My Throne.

I am your Father.

I am your Life.

I am the Beginning of no beginning.

I am the End of no end.

I alone am Life.

All that is is Mine for I AM.

I love what I create.

I love My dear children.

When they call to Me I respond.

Woe to those dear little ones of mine who do not call to me for I am humble.

When My little ones turn from Me I call them again and again.

I lure them. I woo them.

My Heart dies of abandonment as My beloved Jesus showed all of
You when my little ones run from me.

I have made you free little ones. Free to choose Me or to deny Me.

When you refuse Me My beloved little ones, you choose death.

While there is time, call to Me.

Come to Me.

Persevere in Me, in My ways oh beautiful children of Mine.

Soon we shall all make merry at the Wedding Feast of the Lamb.

O Bride of My Son, how beautiful you are!

How pleased I am with your preparations.

Thousands and thousands prepare night and day.

Each prayer is an ornament at the Feast.

Each renounced appetite of the world is a garment of such
Splendor that My children shall exalt forever at its sight.

Little ones, pray now and fast now.

Persevere My little ones.

FOOTNOTES

CHAPTER 1: APPARITIONS: REIGN OF LOVE

1. Father Rene Laurentin, Apparitions of the Blessed Virgin Mary, Veritas Publications, Dublin, 1990 (p.19)
2. Ibid.
3. Statement of Pope Leo XIII.
4. Fatima is also the name of the prophet Mohammed's daughter. He was known to have said that the Blessed Virgin Mary is the highest ranking woman in heaven. He said his daughter Fatima ranks second.
5. Jan Connell, Queen of the Cosmos, Paraclete Press, Orleans, Mass., 1990., and Janice T. Connell, Visions of the Children, St. Martins Press, N.Y. 1992, for information concerning the secrets for the world disclosed to the visionaries at Medjugorje by the Blessed Virgin Mary.
6. John Haffert, To Prevent This, 101 Foundation, Asbury, N.J. 1993 p.53.
7. Janice T. Connell, Visions of the Children, Op. Cit. Ivan Interview.
8. Letter of Lucia, 18 May 1936, Documents p. 413. as quoted in John Haffert, To Prevent This, p. 53.
9. Author's interview with Marija Pavlovic, Jan. 25, 1988. Medjugorje.

CHAPTER 2: VICTORIOUS QUEEN OF THE WORLD

1. John Haffert, Finally Russia, 101 Foundation, Asbury Parl, N.J. 1993 p.32.
2. Ibid.
3. Christopher Rengers, O.F.M. Cap. The Youngest Phophet, Alba House, N.Y. 1986. pp. 113.114.
4. Rev. Anselm Burke, O.C.D.: Scapular Press N.Y. 1956 p. 91.
5. Ibid. p. 93.
6. John Haffert, Finally Russia, Op. Cit. p. 32.
7. Ibid.
8. Ibid p. 16.
9. Ibid.

CHAPTER 3: PARIS

1. Interior words not from a human source.
2. Ibid.
3. John Haffert, Finally Russia, Op. Cit. 1993, p. 22.
4. Ibid.
5. See p.p. 8, 12 Supra.
6. Ibid. p. 23.

CHAPTER 5: LISIEUX

1. Author's interview with Peace Pilgrim Dolores M. Dorsey.

CHAPTER 6: FATIMA

1. Christopher Rengers, O.F.M. Cap. Op. Cit. p. 19.

2. Ibid.
3. Ibid. pp 32,33.
4. Ibid p. 35.
5. Msgr. Peter Mimnagh Pastor, San Diego, CA.
6. Rengers, Op. Cit., p. 34.
7. Ibid, p. 37.
8. Ibid, p. 38.
9. Ibid, p. 42.
10. Ibid
11. Ibid, pp 54,55.
12. Ibid, p. 57.
13. Ibid, p. 58,59.
14. Ibid, p. 60.
15. Ibid
16. Ibid, p.62
17. Ibid
18. Personal interview by author with Sister Agnes Sassacawa and others at Akita, Japan 1991.
19. John Haffert, To Prevent This, 101 Foundation, N.J. 1993 p. 5.
20. Personal interview by author with Ivan Dragicevic during The Gulf War, January, 1991, in Washington, D.C.

CHAPTER 7: PRAGUE

1. John Haffert, Finally Russia, Op. Cit. p. 45.
2. Author's interview with Peace Pilgrim Lee Bowers.

CHAPTER 8: MOSCOW

1. Author's interview with John Haffert.
2. Author's interview with John Haffert.
3. Negotiations for this historic encounter were conducted by delegates of the Episcopal Community of Jesus of Orleans, Mass. whose choir, Gloriae Dei Cantores had sung in Russia, in Moscow Cathedral, the preceeding Easter. David Manuel represented the community at the meeting with the Patriarch.
4. Author's interview with John Haffert.
5. Author's interview with John Haffert.
6. Author's interview with John Haffert.

CHAPTER 9: POLAND

1. Rev. John S. Gulez, The Most Famous Shrines of the Blessed Virgin in the World, privately printed, at Reading, PA. 1947, p.63
2. Author's interview with John Haffert.
3. Author's interview with Peace Pilgrim Mary Anne King.
4. Author's interview with John Haffert.
5. Author's interview with Brother Leonard Konopke, Marian Spirituality Center, Brookville, MD.
6. Sister M. Faustina Kowalska, Divine Mercy in My Soul, Marian Press: Stockbridge, Mass. 1987, p.28.

APPENDIX 1

Prayer To Our Lady of Fatima For Russia

Hail! Mother of God, star more brilliant than the sun!

Hail! Mother of God, spreading joy over the earth!

Hail! O reconciler of fallen Adam!

Hail! Consoler of tears of Eve!

Blessed are You, O dispenser of gifts of God,

For the innumerable graces which You pour upon the entire world

And for those which, for centuries, You have so prodigiously granted
 to the Christians of Russia.

We confide, we entrust into Your hands the destiny of Russia.

We plead with You Immaculate Heart, not only for those who have the
 happiness of knowing and loving You Divine Son,

And those who know that they have in Heaven a powerful Mother,

But also for all those souls who live far from God,
 and from You...

Shower upon the Russian nation graces of light,
 graces of fire,

Irresistible Graces like those which transformed Saul into St. Paul.

We beg you in union with all the saints of the Russian land,

With all the priests and faithful who died there,
 martyrs for Christ,

With millions of Russian Christians who so love and venerate You,

With all those who continue to pray before Your Icons.

United with them we pray...

No one has ever had recourse to You in vain.

Therefore we are certain that You will hear us,

That you will not delay in taking pity upon the world and on Russia

That this beloved nation be free to follow Your luminous path,

To proclaim the blessings of God,

To work under Your orders, oh Victorious Leader,

Together to establish the Reign of Christ in the World

Until that day when, all are united around You,
 with vibrant hearts we shall glorify God forever.

YOUTH CONGRESS AT FATIMA.
May 13, 1947